Scalar Heart Connection™

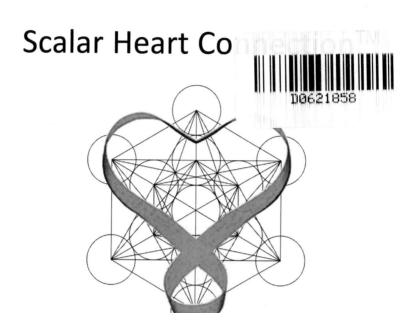

Stephen Linsteadt

Natural Healing House Press

ISBN: 978-09741123-2-9
Library of Congress Control Number: 2012905320

The information contained in this book is intended for research and educational purposes only. The author does not
present any part of this work, directly or indirectly, for the
diagnoses or prescription of any disease or condition. People
who use the information from this book are advised to take
responsibility for consulting the health professional of their
choice regarding all matters pertaining to their physical, emotional or mental health.

Cover Design by Davood Mantegh
Editorial and Interior Design by Indiana Jane Linsteadt

Printed and bound in the United States

Published by Natural Healing House Press
La Quinta, California
www.NaturalHealingHouse.com
1 3 5 7 9 8 6 4 2

Dedicated to
Maria Elena

Acknowledgements

I am deeply grateful to all my teachers and advisors, who have helped me along the way of assimilating this information and understanding, particularly Chloe Faith Wordsworth, Ardis Osborn, Kam Yuen, James Oschman, Martin Keymer, and Noelle A. Rose. I would also like to acknowledge the work and inspiration of Fritz-Albert Popp, Valerie Hunt, Candace Pert, Hans Jenny, Bruce Lipton, and Amit Goswami. Additionally, I want to thank my life-long friend, Steve Nathan, for his mental clarity and deep insights along the way. Beverly Lenz contributed to the organization of this process. I am grateful to E. J. Spevak for her insights and support. This work has materialized because of the unending tireless support and ever-present heart of Maria Elena Boekemeyer.

Contents

"The intuitive mind is a sacred gift and the rational mind is a faithful servant. We have created a society that honors the servant and has forgotten the gift."
~ Albert Einstein

Introduction

Our inexhaustible desire for money, power, companionship, or recognition can lead to a life of imbalance. A stressful climb up the corporate ladder took its toll on my first marriage and then on my physical and mental health. My cells reacted to a prolonged divorce process by contracting defensively based on their 'perception' that our collective self (all 60 to 90 trillion cells that make up 'me') was threatened. This 'perception' led to mental and physical exhaustion, but also to a journey towards a new understanding; that we are pulsating fields of frequency vibrations. It opened my mind-brain to the possibility that I could change and that my perception was only a program from the past.

Our life experiences often lead us to a point where it becomes necessary to seek a change in behavior and our long-held beliefs. Who is not seeking some change in at least one aspect of their life? Thanks to the events at that time in my life, I discovered that change is possible when I realized that all my thoughts, feelings, and problems are frequency vibrations, and that frequencies can shift into phase with what is life enhancing. It is possible to change the frequencies of our mind-brain reactions with our conscious awareness. It is a question of intention. Similar to changing the radio station we listen to habitually, we can change what we believe. It is a matter of changing what we think about, as well as the habit of how we think. Sometimes, we need a little help.

The evolutionary challenge we all face lies in how we strike equilibrium with the outside frequencies that bombard us each day in the 'real' world. But what if we are not able to achieve such a balance due to worry, upset, or other negative emotions? When we are unable to access our inner dialogue, we compromise our ability to respond with equanimity to the disharmonious frequencies on the outside. We attempt to reach that calm inner balance, but our overactive mind remains stuck in emotional reactions and old behavior patterns we acquired through the influences of childhood. We mostly see life through the lens of these earlier experiences. We are generally unaware of the source of our emotional reactions as they arise from suppressed subconscious material. The result is that we experience unease, anxiety, worry or other energy depleting responses.

My personal journey led me to many teachers, who helped me peel through many layers of old subconscious mind-brain circuit patterns. They taught that knowledge is often an obstacle to understanding. Knowledge derived from societal beliefs and sensory perceptions can block understanding. Our accumulated knowledge is based on what we have experienced through our senses and from what our parents, teachers, and history books tell us. On the other hand, when our heart carries us to the depths of perfect understanding, then thought-forms, perceptions, feelings, and self-awareness dissolve from consciousness. Consciousness then slips through our entanglement with matter and merges with the Infinite like a grain of salt dissolving in the ocean.

Albert Einstein warned us that we have given mastery of our lives to the reigns of mind-brain consciousness. He encouraged us to re-connect with heart-consciousness, which flows intuitively out of the interconnected fabric of spacetime.

C. G. Jung referred to the higher intelligence of Universal Consciousness when he asked us to "consider synchronistic phenomena, premonitions, and dreams that come true."[1] He explained that Infinite Intelligence has other ways "of informing us of things which by all logic we could not possi-

---

1 Jung, C G, *Memories, Dreams, Reflections*, (Vintage Books, 1989), p. 302

bly know."[2] One way Universal Consciousness informs us is through the rhythmic beating of our heart.

The heart synchronizes to the heartbeat of the Earth, Sun, Galaxy, and beyond. When we tune in to heart-consciousness, we open ourselves to information, inspiration, and creative insights. We tune in to the heartbeat of the Cosmos. The heart's rhythmic songs of Universal Consciousness washes over every cell in our body, coupling with our brain waves as it radiates out to everyone around us.

The heart can give us that little extra help we sometimes need to re-align ourselves with what is positive and life enhancing. One way to communicate with the wisdom of the heart is through a method called Scalar Heart Connection™. The heart is the interface between mind-brain consciousness and Universal Consciousness. Heart-centered consciousness helps to bring us into greater harmony within ourselves and with the planet as a whole. Joseph Campbell said, "The heart is the organ of opening up to somebody else."[3] Scalar Heart Connection™ helps us open to our own heart. When our own heart is open, we are able to open up to the hearts of others. Imagine a planet of people with open hearts, connected to the wellbeing of each other and the health of the planet. It can happen. It is already happening.

---

2 Ibid.

3 Campbell J with Moyers B, *The Power of Myth*, (Anchor Books, 1991), p. 234

Vibration Gives Rise to Things

Many say that life entered the human body by the help of
music,
but the truth is that life itself is music.
~ Hafiz

Normally, because of old patterns or social conditioning, we limit our perspective to the viewpoint of mind-brain
consciousness. When I use the word 'consciousness' I am re-
ferring to 'self-awareness.' This is not a complete definition,
but it is a place to start. The critical paradigm shift is to view
consciousness as the foundation of matter, not the other way
around.[4] If we can change this perspective, we will understand that Universal Consciousness works first through the
heart. The heart only later communicates with mind-brain
when action is required. Understanding what the heart is
connected to requires that we drop the notion that matter
consists of 'things.' The heart is connected to the energy that
commingles into 'things.' Einstein forced us to re-think our
Newtonian paradigm that matter and 'things' consists of hard
particles. He gave us a new definition of reality. He defined
Universe as a field of energy.

Unfortunately, Einstein did not specifically define 'energy.' He warned us that our concepts are limited because we
rely on the mind-brain for interpretation. He said our quest to
understand reality is like someone trying to understand the
mechanism of a closed watch. We see the face of the watch

4 Goswami A, *The Self-Aware Universe; How Consciousness Creates the Material
World*, (G. P. Putnam's Sons, 1993)

and the moving hands. We may even develop instruments to detect its ticking; however, since we are unable to open the case, we will never be able to compare our concept with the reality of the mechanism. He doubted that we would even be able to imagine the possibility of the meaning of such a comparison.[5]

At our current level of scientific understanding, it appears that energy is a self-organizing field of vibration. Vibrations occur at all times in all atoms, molecules, and cells. All energy transactions, therefore, have different kinds of resonance. David Bohm, quantum physicist and philosopher, speculated that 'active information' is an energy form acting to 'inform' or direct energy into larger forms. He used the term 'in-form,' which he said is actively putting form into something or to imbue something with form.[6] This implies the existence of cosmic intelligence, suggesting the heart is connected to the energy of the universe, which is omnipresent and omnipotent 'active information.' I recognized this as the metaphysical philosophy of the East, which says that pure Infinite Consciousness, in the beginning of creation, appeared in whatever form it chose to manifest itself.[7] Said differently, the distinction between the essence of one substance and another arises only due to the intelligence identifying itself as different.[8] This is equivalent to one energy form looking at another energy form and thinking 'other.'

I liked Buckminster Fuller's explanation of consciousness. He was a pioneer in global thinking. He defined consciousness to mean an awareness of otherness. The beginning

5 Einstein A, Leopold I, *The Evolution of Physics*, (Touchstone, 1967), p. 31
6 Bohm D, Basil, J. Hiley, *The Undivided Universe: An Ontological Interpretation of Quantum Theory*, (Routledge; reprint edition, 1995), p. 35
7 Venkatesananda S, *The Concise Yoga Vasistha*, (State University of New York Press, 1985), p. 68
8 Venkatesananda S, *The Concise Yoga Vasistha*, (State University of New York Press, 1985), p. 68

of 'life,' he said, always imposes a minimum of one restraint: without otherness there is nothing to observe, hence, no awareness, only nothingness.[9] He also defined Universe as "the aggregate of all humanity's consciously apprehended and communicated non-simultaneous and only partially overlapping experiences."[10] Unfortunately for most of us, Fuller tended to complicate the complicated by his choice of words. He also liked to communicate with verbs, which is why he refers to Universe instead of 'the' Universe. I like that point of view. It removes Universe and Earth from the noun of 'things.' Fuller liked to get away from nouns in order to honor the realization by modern science that there are no 'things,' only events he called "mathematical behaviors of energy phenomena."[11] All of which, he said, subjective or objective, can be defined by angle and frequency modulations in respect to human consciousness.[12] This definition allows us to view the beating heart as a frequency modulator. As such, it is at the center of the energy phenomena that surrounds us. More accurately, it is inseparable from that energy phenomenon. As Fuller concluded, "To each of us, Universe must be all that isn't me, plus me."[13]

For Fuller, Universe meant "toward one-ness," implying a minimum of twoness.[14] He described Universe as progressively revealing, where "Humanity can only evolve toward cosmic totality. . ."[15] In the process, we are encumbered with our sensory perceptions of Universe. Bohm suggested that the very act of interpreting Universe also creates Universe. "Through our meanings we change nature's be-

9 Buckminster Fuller R, *Synergetics: Explorations in the Geometry of Thinking*, (Macmillan Publishing Company, 1978), p. 103
10 Ibid., p. 81
11 Ibid., p. 71
12 Ibid., p. 83
13 Ibid.
14 Ibid.
15 Ibid., p. 84, 85

ing. "[People's] meaning-making capacity turns [them] into nature's partner, a participant in shaping her evolution."[16] If 'meaning' is derived from mind-brain perceptions arising from our senses, a re-focus on heart-consciousness may lead us to a perception of the true nature of our being. As we have seen, both the mind and matter are vibrating aspects of the same thing. I believe this is the key to why the Sufis felt the human heart is the interface between the body and the 'other world.'[17] Said differently, the heart is the interface between pure being and the illusion of separate identity. It is often our sense of separateness that causes our emotional vicissitudes.

Disconnection from our heart, which is connected to pure Infinite consciousness, causes us to rely on mind-brain reactions to emotional stimuli. The mind-brain then attempts to make meaning out of emotions and reacts with a host of neuropeptides and other 'fight or flight' chemicals instead of responding from heart-consciousness. This leads to reactions based on response conditioning, leading to anger, upset, and a further loss of connection with our true state of being. My question was how to re-connect with our heart in order to respond to life's challenges with heart-consciousness. I discovered that it starts with understanding that heart-consciousness is a field of energy vibration.

---

16 Weber R, ed., Dialogues *With Scientists & Sages: the Search for Unity*, (Routledge and Kegan Paul, 1986), p. 18
17 Shabistari M, Trans. Robert Abdul Hayy Darr, *Garden of Mystery* (*Gulshan-I rāz*), (Archetype, 2007), p. 204

Love Resonance

The heart is the hub of all sacred places.
Go there and roam.
~ Bhagawan Nityananda

If the heart is the mediator between the vibrations of the Infinite and the oscillations that commingle into matter, then we can view spacetime as the medium or the ether. "But this ether," said Einstein, "may not be thought of as endowed with the quality characteristic of ponderable media."[18] Physicist Milo Wolff referred to it as 'space resonance' to indicate that all matter is comprised of waves propagating in the medium of space.[19] Recent discoveries of 'dark matter' and 'dark energy' have caused Western scientists to acknowledge the existence of an unseen energy medium or 'quantum medium.' Milo Wolff called it 'space resonance' because the term 'resonance' also refers to a standing wave. Resonance is the language of the heart. Resonance is a vibration whose specific signature can stimulate emotional response centers in our body-mind. The guiding principle of the Scalar Heart Connection™ process is the 'tapping into' the resonance of our emotional imbalances. The key to how we accomplish this is to realize that everything in Universe is a resonance pattern or standing wave energy event.

French physicist Louis de Broglie was the first to notice

---

18 Einstein A, *Sidelights on Relativity*, An address delivered on May 5, 1920, in the University of Leyden, Kessinger Publishing, p. 10-11
19 Wolff M, *Exploring the Physics of the Unknown Universe*, (Technotran Press, 1990), p. 178

the standing wave nature of the electron model proposed at that time by Niels Bohr. He said:

> The determination of the stable motions of the electrons in the atom involves whole numbers, and so far the only phenomena in which whole numbers were involved in physics were those of interference and of normal modes of vibration. This fact suggested to me the idea that electrons too could not be regarded simply as particles, but that frequency (wave properties) must be assigned to them also.[20]

The traditional example of a standing wave is the movement of a violin string. The wave of a vibrating string is reflected back and forth at both ends of the string. Unlike a typical moving wave, the two reflecting waves on the string intersect at evenly spaced intervals creating 'nodes' or points of no movement. The number of nodes will increase as the frequency increases by whole octave or harmonic intervals. De Broglie imagined these whole number intervals as standing waves of specific frequencies related to certain orbits of the electron about the proton.

It was Erwin Schrödinger who later discovered that these standing waves are scalar waves rather than vector waves. Vector waves, like electromagnetic waves, have both a direction and amplitude. Scalar waves have amplitude without a directional component. Examples of a scalar field include the distribution of temperature in space or the pressure distribution in a fluid. In a room where the temperature is the same from one corner to another, only one reading is required to give information about the rest of the field. This

---

20 de Broglie L, *The Wave Nature of the Electron*, Nobel Lecture, December 12, 1929

Love Resonance

gives a sense of a homogeneous information field and lends itself to certain geometric properties. Einstein said the de Broglie-Schrödinger approach had a certain sense of the character of a field theory, and does indeed deduce the existence of only discrete states (standing waves). He said it does so on the basis of differential equations applying a kind of resonance argument.[21]

Milo Wolff describes resonance as a love affair between two instruments.[22] When the standing waves of two instruments have the same frequency, sound energy can be transferred between them.[23] This is seen in the example where the note of 'A' on a piano will cause the 'A' string on a nearby guitar to vibrate. The strings of the two instruments are in sympathetic vibration or resonance with each other. Wolff's Space Resonance Theory describes spherical wave resonances occurring in the fabric of space.[24] Accordingly, the 'particles' of matter are spherical oscillators containing an "IN" wave towards the center and an "OUT" wave moving away from the center. The two waves are of the same frequency and therefore, like the violin string, come together to form a standing wave.[25]

Every 'atom' is comprised of various kinds of resonances. The more complicated the structure, the more frequencies are involved. When two elements are in a state of vibrational and harmonic affinity (resonant coupling), identical energy patterns pass between them, even across distances.[26] Resonance coupling is a kind of love resonance.

---

21 Einstein A, *Ideas and Opinions*, (Broadway, 1995), p. 285
22 Wolff M, *Exploring the Physics of the Unknown Universe*, (Technotran Press, 1990), p. 114
23 Ibid., p. 114
24 Ibid., p. 180
25 Ibid.
26 Lawlor R, *Homage to Pythagoras: Rediscovering Sacred Science*, (Lindisfarne Books, 1994), p. 46

Scalar Heart Connection™

Love resonance happens when you think of a friend and moments later they call. Love resonance happens when the "OUT" waves of our thoughts are coherent and match the frequency of what we want to attract into our lives. We are frequency oscillators and the waves of our thoughts propagate infinitely in the medium of spacetime. This helps explain why positive thinking is important and why it is not always the answer to manifesting our ideal reality. It helps explain why positive affirmations are helpful and why they do not always lead to lasting positive effects. The reason has to do with resonance coupling. Wolff's model demonstrates that we have to resonate with what we want to attract. We have to become the thing we want right down to the exact frequency oscillation. Often, we may think we resonate with our goals and ambitions, but subconsciously we may be harboring small doubts. These small doubts and negative beliefs sneak in and create chaotic interference waves through our otherwise positive intentions.

The most impressive illustration of how positive resonance can manifest in our lives was presented by Jeff Volk at a Resonance Repatterning Association seminar I attended in the early nineties. This was my first introduction to the scientific study of how vibration creates matter and I was extremely fortunate to discover the work of physician and natural scientist, Hans Jenny (1904-1972). Jenny is the founder of Cymatics, the study of wave phenomena. The following chapter explains how this information changed my perspective of how I view and react to the world.

Vibration Creates Geometry

If we can comprehend the wholeness of vibration or oscillation, and grasp the totalities in which it is manifested, then we have caught hold of reality.
~ Hans Jenny[27]

Jenny said it is not a question of needing more sophisticated apparati or experimental designs but rather he urged us to develop our faculties of observation, perception, and insight.[28]

Following the work of German physicist, Ernst Chladni and his research into the modes of vibration on a mechanical surface, Jenny experimented with animating colloidal suspensions in liquids with musical tones. In his experiments using droplets of water, the outward moving waves reflect off the outer membrane and pass through the source wave in phase. This creates the appearance of a static geometric pattern, or standing wave, even though the particles in the water are vibrating and flowing (figure 1). Volk emphasizes the importance of this demonstration as it shows how the oscillating standing wave spheres of our micro-world orient and bond with one another. It also explains the "massive oscillations of gravitational fields in galactic interactions."[29]

Jenny found that certain frequencies resulted in equally spaced nodes or wave-troughs and anti-nodes (wave-peaks).

---

27 Jenny H, *Cymatics Volume 2*, (Basilius Presse, 1974), p. 183
28 Ibid.
29 Volk J, *From Vibration to Manifestation: Assuming our Rightful Place in Creation*, The Quester; Autumn 2010, p. 4

Scalar Heart Connection™

The predominant shape was the hexagon with its interlaced triangles; the Star-Tetrahedron (figure 1).[30] Jenny describes that rotary waves often emerge and set the whole pattern of harmonic oscillations turning in a screw-like path – a spiral.[31] Jenny's work provides visualization to Einstein's notion that what we think of as a particle is actually a localized vibration or pulse emerging from a field, like a vortex forming in a flowing stream.[32]

Fig. 1. Hans Jenny, Cymatics Volume 2
(Courtesy: MACROmedia Publishing)

The various geometric forms Jenny created by frequency held their shape as long as the pitch remained constant. As soon as the pitch or frequency was changed, the form dissolved into chaos. As the pitch increased to a specific level, a new and more complex form would emerge. This helped me understand how the apparent chaos that materializes in my life is merely transitional and necessary. In order to manifest higher ideals, I am sometimes forced to let go of worn-out

30 Jenny H, *Cymatics Volume 2*, (Basilius Presse, 1974), p. 97
31 Ibid., p. 169
32 Bohm D, edited by Lee Nichol, *The Essential David Bohm*, (Routledge, 2007), p. 3

Vibration Creates Geometry

parental and ancestral patterns, societal beliefs, or other non-serving thought-forms and allow these patterns to dissolve into chaos before new positive patterns can materialize. It is also possible that chaos is a manifestation of indecisiveness on my part. Perhaps I intend to create something positive in my life, but I am stuck in fears, worries, or other negative behavior patterns. Jenny's experiments show the power of our thoughts and feelings and how we can create or dissolve the reality around us based on the vibrations we put out into the world.

Jenny noticed the propensity of the Tetrahedron to form at the center of the oscillating spheres (see figure 1). He said the phenomenon echoes the words of Plato's Timaeus, the Pythagorean, who tells us in detail how Universe is built up from innumerable triangles. The basic tenet of Pythagorean philosophy is that form, as well as time, imitates eternity and revolves according to a law of number.[33] Number is frequency – vibration and musical intervals. Jenny says Plato uses the character Timaeus to describe the creation of Universe in accordance with musical intervals. Timaeus explains how the Platonic solids are generated from Tetrahedrons and how they all spring up from one.[34] Timaeus also describes how each form, nested one in the other, rotates independently of one another in counter rotations as observed by Jenny. Jenny explains, "These 'clouds of electrons' such as the atomic physicist describes are oscillatory systems ordered according to proportions, number and symmetry."[35] Nature reveals this underlying rhythm in patterns of rhythmicity in the formation of plant and animal tissue, from cell division, vertebrae aggregations, to the cycles of the seasons and planets from which we derive our perception of time.[36]

---

33 Plato, *Timaeus*, par. 38a
34 Ibid., par. 54c-d
35 Jenny H, *Cymatics Volume 2*, (Basilius Presse, 1974), p. 161
36 Ibid., p. 165-166

Scalar Heart Connection™

Timaeus tells us that motion never exists in what is uniform.[37] Jenny's standing wave patterns show us that without the crests and troughs of the waves there is nothing to perceive as form. Timaeus says this inequality in wave patterns is what causes nature to seek uniformity.[38] This is the origin of polar opposites: crest and trough; light and dark; matter and anti-matter; high notes and low notes. In keeping with Eastern spiritual traditions, we see that solidness and separateness (duality) are illusions. There is only unity at the fundamental level of Universe. Jenny helps us understand that Universe is in motion and this motion strives for equilibrium. As Timaeus explains, it is hard to conceive that anything can move without a mover.[39] This is the challenge with trying to understand the inner workings of a closed watch case. We don't understand what it is that is causing the movement nor do we know exactly what it is that is moving. As George Bernard Shaw said in his address at a dinner for Albert Einstein, "Science can never solve one problem without raising ten more problems."[40]

---

37 Plato, *Timaeus*, par. 57e
38 Ibid., par. 58a
39 Ibid., par. 57e
40 Einstein A, *Einstein on Cosmic Religion and Other Opinions & Aphorisms,*

Vibration Creates Geometry

Heraclitus provided a clue to the mystery when he said it is 'Logos' that orders the whole world.[41] Heraclitus advised that it is wise to acknowledge that all things are one and to listen to the Logos or the 'Word of God.' Likewise, Jenny advised that if we can comprehend the wholeness of vibration, then we have caught hold of reality.[42]

Michio Kaku, co-founder of String Field Theory, proposes that sub-atomic particles are vibrating strings like musical notes on tiny strings.[43] Kaku claims Universe is a symphony of vibrating strings and the mind of God is cosmic music resonating through eleven-dimensional hyperspace.[44] This is appealing because, as he says, we are nothing but cosmic melodies. The ancient East, and I'm thinking of the Egyptians described by Plato in the Republic, as well as the later Essenes (that includes the early Judeo-Christians and later Gnostics), Sufis, Hindus, Kabbalists, Buddhists, and many others all have traditions that mention light and sound as the root cause and sustainer of Universe. Spheres of blazing light and the blare of trumpets is a recurring theme, even in the Bible.

It is not common knowledge that Timaeus was a quantum string theorist. However, if we look closely at his description of the most fundamental level of the Platonic Solids we find that he was indeed describing String Theory. Timaeus describes the most beautiful of all forms as the one of which the double forms a third triangle, which is equilateral having the square of the longer side equal to three times the square of the lesser side (figure 2).[45]

(Dover Publications, 2009), p. 33

41 Heraclitus, *The Complete Fragments*, Trans. and Comments by William Harris, Middlebury College, frag. 64

42 Jenny H, *Cymatics Volume 2*, (Basilius Presse, 1974), p. 183

43 Kaku M, *The Universe is a Symphony of Vibrating Stings*, YouTube, posted by bigthink, 31 May 2011

44 Ibid.

45 Plato, *Timaeus*, par. 54a

Scalar Heart Connection™

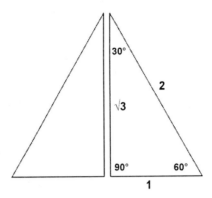

Fig. 2. Timaeus' fundamental form

Fuller treated the strings of string theory as open-ended triangular spirals or an energy event. He said triangles are always positive or negative helixes. Two such triangular strings or 'energy events' create the Tetrahedron; the first Platonic solid (figure 3).[46]

Fig. 3. Two vibrating strings (energy events) create the Tetrahedron

The two opposite spiraling triangle-strings attract each other. They combine to form a Tetrahedron (figure 3 – far right); the fundamental form described by Timaeus. These dual energy currents are Yin and Yang in Taoist tradition:

46 Buckminster Fuller, R *Synergetics: Explorations in the Geometry of Thinking,* (Macmillan Publishing Company, 1978), p. 4

Vibration Creates Geometry

In other Eastern traditions, there is the concept of the outward and inward currents manifesting in spacetime. Together, they are like the outgoing and incoming breath of the Universe. In Gnostic cosmology, the outgoing spirit descended to the lowest level of creation where it became crystallized. This spirit energy became as dry as dust with hardly any spirituality remaining. It appeared as a mist known to the Gnostics as Maya. Maya threw off exceedingly fine and subtle particles, which became the building blocks of the subatomic particles, atoms and molecules that make up all matter and things of this world. Maya is now without any spiritual energy of her own and must rely solely on the energy she receives from the desires of humankind. On the other hand, the upward current is the power of attraction, which draws the soul up, back to union and wholeness in the higher realms of bliss. Some call it Logos or the Word; the creative power. The intersection of these two currents creates the holographic universe:

These same two energy currents circulate through the body like a caduceus staff, commingling along the spine to form the chakras (more on that later). The dynamics of these currents and how they come together to create form is visible in the example of Jenny's vibratory patterns (figure 1). When I first saw Jenny's figures at Volk's presentation, I was amazed at how the complexity of motion and wave dynamics manifests the dual Tetrahedrons in the center.

The dual Tetrahedrons come together to create eight vertices, which is the cube; the second Platonic solid (figure 4). The third Platonic solid is the Octahedron, which arises from the common area of the two intersecting Tetrahedrons (figure 5).

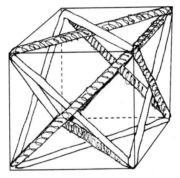

Fig. 4. Cube created by vertices of two interlaced Tetrahedrons

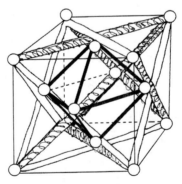

Fig. 5. Octahedron nested inside dual Tetrahedrons

Vibration Creates Geometry

Thanks to Jenny, I could visualize atoms as geometric patterns of flowing energy. Changes in the rate of vibration increases the complexity of the flow and the geometricity. Each Platonic shape forms two spheres; one circumscribed by its vertices ('protons'), as seen in the figure above, and another inscribed within its faces. The inscribed sphere becomes the circumscribed sphere of a smaller nested structure, and so on. In this model of the atom as inward and outward going spherical waves, the space between the inscribed and circumscribed spheres is the "electron cloud" described in the standard model. For more information about the geometry of the periodic table, refer to the Appendix.

When looking at atoms in terms of geometry, I came upon the carbon atom, which is the atom essential to all carbon-based life forms on Earth. One cannot avoid the dual nature of carbon. The atom organizes itself loosely as graphite; a very soft and slippery substance. Carbon is also capable of organizing itself, under the right conditions, into a tetrahedral matrix known as the diamond. On one hand, carbon as graphite is common and fragile. On the other, carbon as a diamond is durable, sublime, and extremely valuable. The tetrahedral matrix of the diamond is a fractal organization of Timaeus' Tetrahedron:

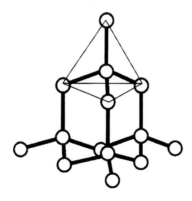

An array of four Tetrahedrons makes clear the fractal nature of the Tetrahedron as the matrix seemingly extends indefinitely as a series of ever expanding Tetrahedrons:

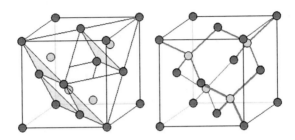

Sets of four Tetrahedrons from the carbon diamond matrix fit inside a square.

If we focus only on the negative space between the Tetrahedrons an Octahedron can be seen:

The Octahedron lies within the 'empty' space of the Tetrahedrons.

Psychologist C. G. Jung used the image of the Octahedron as a double pyramid to symbolize the dual nature of consciousness.[47] The Egyptians might have also utilized the Octahedron in the pyramid to represent the Higher Self in opposition to the lower self:

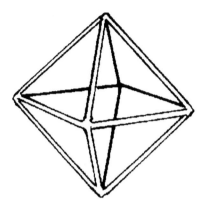

The model of the atom as a spherical Tetrahedron standing wave reveals the underlying order of number through its geometry. Spheres that resonate in phase "attract" one another. If all matter is a fractal of the same omni-directional poly-tetrahedral matrix, then it makes sense that all 'matter' is attracted to each other. The law of attraction now takes on a new meaning. We attract whatever our heart is counting, in resonance with, or that with which it is in phase. "Wherever our heart is, that is where our treasure manifests."[48]

Jung believed that 'number' itself is an archetype; a symbol of an underlying principle of wholeness and unity. As such, it is the most basic element of matter.[49] He felt that number is the most fitting tool our mind can employ for the apprehension of an already existing order.[50] He said, "It may well

47 Jung C G, *Aion; Researches Into the Phenomenology of the Self*, Bollingen Series, CW 9 Vol. II, (Routledge & Kegan Paul, 1959). See Chapter: "The Structure and Dynamics of the Self."
48 *Matthew* 6:21
49 von Franz M, *Number and Time*, (Northwestern University Press, 1998), p. 45
50 Jung C G, *Synchronicity: An Acausal Connecting Principle*, Collective Works

be the most primitive element of order in the human mind . . . thus we define number psychologically as an archetype of order which has become conscious."[51]

When our mind distinguishes one thing from another, it is essentially counting. However, researchers at the Institute of HeartMath demonstrated that the heart receives 'intuitive' information before the brain. This supports other research showing that the nervous system within the heart continuously sends signals to "higher brain centers involved in perception, cognition, and emotional processing."[52] This helped me understand that if 'number' is the bridge between the physically knowable and the realm of intuition or metaphysical knowing, then it is the heart that is at the heart of counting 'number.'

The process of Scalar Heart Connection™ utilizes the geometry of the Tetrahedron as a means of accessing the heart's intuition. When we are not in resonance or in phase with what we want to attract, it is the heart that holds the secret to what outside influences are standing between us and our goals. In the next chapter, we will examine more closely the geometry of number, which holds the key to unlocking our highest potential.

Volume 8, (Bollingen Foundation, second edition, 1969) par. 870, p. 456
51 Ibid.
52 McCraty R, *The Resonant Heart*, Shift: At the Frontiers of Consciousness, Dec. 2004 / Feb 2005, p.15

The Geometry of Number

There is geometry in the humming of the strings,
there is music in the spacing of the spheres.
~ Pythagoras

It was Timaeus who earlier pointed us in the direction of how Universe springs up from the One into myriad fractals of Tetrahedrons according to the law of number and musical vibration. Timaeus also explained that the 'forms of time,' which imitates eternity, revolves according to a law of number. He said eternity itself rests in unity. The 'forms of time,' therefore, is only a copy.[53] The idea that the physical plane is a copy of the heavenly plane is an ancient idea. We already know Timaeus was a Pythagorean. Pythagoras had ties with the Egyptians. This explains Timaeus's reference to Hermes later on in the dialogue. In the Hermetic Texts, which are later Greek borrowings from Ancient Egyptian scripture passed down from the god Thoth (the Greek equivalent of Hermes), we find the dictum, "As above, so below," from Thoth-Hermes explaining to his disciple, Asclepius:[54]

> Do you not know, Asclepius, that Egypt is an image
> of heaven? Or, to speak more exactly, in Egypt all the

53 Plato, *Timaeus*, par. 37a – 38b
54 Mahé J, "Preliminary Remarks on the Demotic "Book of Thoth" and the Greek Hermetica" Vigiliae Christianae 50.4 (1996:353-363) p.358f. "There are many parallels with Egyptian prophecies, with hymns to the gods or other mythological texts, and with direct allusions, the closest comparisons can be found in Egyptian wisdom literature, characteristically couched in words of advice from a "father" to a "son".

operations of the powers which rule and work in
heaven have been transferred down to earth below?[55]

Thus Pythagoras and Moses, who had associations
with Egypt, suggest a common origin of the two geometric
traditions stemming from the Essenes and influencing Hellenistic thought and later Kabbalah traditions.[56] The symbol
of the mirror imaging of heaven and Earth is portrayed by
the upward pointing triangle and the downward pointing triangle (figure 8).

The Great Symbol of Solomon

Fig. 8. "Quod Superius Macroprosopus, Quod Inferius
Microprosopus."
It is equivalent to the Latin phrase:
'Quod superius sicut quot inferius'
which means: 'As above, so below.'

---

55 *Hermetica*, Asclepius III, (Solos Press ed.), p. 136
56 Leet L, *The Secret Doctrine of the Kabbalah*, (Inner Traditions, 1999), p. 8

The Geometry of Number

In many ancient texts on the subject, these interlaced triangles represent the spiritual and material universes linked together in the constitution of the human being, who has the qualities of both Nature and Divinity.[57] The six-pointed star is also found in Hindu temples and shrines, where it is considered a symbol of harmony between spirit and matter.[58] Some North American Indian tribes have also used the hexagram as a symbol for the union of spirit and matter.[59] Later, we will explore the Indian system of yoga and its graphic representation of the six-pointed star as the heart chakra. This representation makes the heart chakra the connecting link between the lower 'carnal' chakras and the three upper 'spiritual' chakras (figure 9).[60]

Fig. 9. Indian yoga heart chakra symbol.

The symbol of the interlaced Tetrahedrons is also a mandala. Mandala is a Sanskrit word that means 'circle.' The basic form of most Hindu and Buddhist mandalas is a square around a circle with a center point. Mandalas may be used to focus attention as a way to establish a sacred space, an aid

57 Hall M, *The Secret Teachings of All Ages: An Encyclopedic Outline of Masonic, Hermetic, Qabbalistic and Rosicrucian Symbolical Philosophy*, (CreateSpace, 2011), p. 42

58 Eder A, *The Star of David: an ancient symbol of integration*, (R. Mass, 1987), p. 22

59 Ibid., p. 23

60 Ibid., p.22

to meditation, or to tap into other realms of knowing. From Jung's experience with his patients, he believed that the unconscious, with the help of dreams, produces the natural symbol of the mandala to signify wholeness and a union of opposites.[61] These inner conflicts often emerged in Jung's patients through dreams. It was the similarity of dream images, between his patients, that caused him to insightfully determine the existence of a common link between all humankind. This common language, of unconscious dream images, is what led him to identify the "Collective Unconscious." He could clearly see a set of common images, or archetypal images, that the subconscious projects in dreams, providing clues to the nature of the inner, hidden conflict.

When Jung painted mandalas himself, he saw them as a record of the self actively working towards wholeness. Ultimately, he felt that all mandalas point to the center or to the unity of the self, as the fragmentary parts of the illusory self make their way to the outer edges. He realized in the mandalas that all of his experiences and all the steps he had taken were all leading back to a single point.[62]

The beauty of the mandala symbol is that it represents our journey back to wholeness or harmony with Infinity. We often find ourselves on the outer edges of our inner mandala, where we encounter conflicts and problems in our lives. However, these conflicts can often be evolutionary vehicles urging us to higher conscious awareness. It is this urging that pulls us towards the center of our inner mandala. Often, as soon as we have seemingly solved one problem, another wave of dissatisfaction begins to take over. In this way, we are never satisfied. This process leads us from one layer along the spiral of unfoldment to the next. For many, this can be a cause of great anxiety and restlessness. Not aware of the process, we may

---

61 Jung C G, *Psychology and Religion*, Bollingen Series XX (Princeton University Press, 1969), par. 150

62 Jung C G, *Memories, Dreams, Reflections*, (Vintage Books, 1989), p. 196

The Geometry of Number

try to cover up our inner conflicts with a variety of antidepressants and other mind-numbing substances. The problem with the 'numbing' approach is that it only causes the unconscious to attempt to reach the individual by even more drastic means, such as an accident, loss of a job, divorce, illness, etc.

I had to learn this the hard way. I spent many happy years on the outside edges of my mandala. Then one day in 1991, my marriage unexpectedly ended. I was rudely urged towards the center of my inner mandala. I began an introspection that continued inconclusively through my second marriage. Shortly after my second marriage – the following week in fact – I found myself in a marriage counselor's office. I was 'encouraged' to attend seminars on the separate extraterrestrial origins of men and women. Before it was all over, I came down with an acute appendicitis; at least that is what my medical doctor determined. He admitted there was no definitive test to make the diagnosis a certainty; however, he would be happy to remove my appendix the following morning as a precaution.

Before I went under the scalpel, a friend of mine suggested I see his Chinese doctor. The 'doctor' turned out to be Kam Yuen, a Shaolin Master, specializing in 'energy medicine.' Whatever, I thought. I only cared about the excruciating abdominal pain that prevented me from standing up straight. At his office, the Chinese 'doctor' asked me to resist his effort to pull my outstretched arm to my side. He mumbled a few things, waved his hand up and down my body and said, "How's that?" "How's that!?" I replied. "It's the craziest thing I've ever seen." "No," he said, "I mean, how does your stomach feel, now?" The pain completely disappeared, but I obviously wanted to know how that was possible. He said I was worried about money and that caused a disruption in the otherwise harmonious resonance of my large intestines. The rest of my abdomen no longer recognized the dissonant frequencies coming from my large intestines and that created a kind of organ rejection, hence the pain. He explained that his technique added a positive resonance in my mind-body system around 'money' and my intestines re-integrated into my abdominal symphony.

I had never heard of anything so outrageous before. Yet, I could not get over how I had been in unbearable pain for three days and within five minutes of being with the Shaolin Master, I was pain free. I called my parents. I felt like I was about to tell them I had been abducted by aliens. When my father told me it sounded like something my crazy sister-in-law was doing, I was relieved. My father was a physicist, so when he uses the word 'crazy' it is his way of labeling something he doesn't logically understand or agree with. I called my sister-in-law, who told me about a seminar she had taken and within three days, I was in my car on the way to Arizona to take the same seminar.

That seminar in Resonance Repatterning in 1993 was my first exposure to the idea that the body is more than a bag of bones, blood and guts. It is energy. Immediately thereafter, I read *The Body Electric*, by Robert O. Becker and *The Holographic Universe,* by Michael Talbot. I was so impressed with this new information that I attended lectures and seminars by many scientists, such as Bruce Lipton ("Biology of Belief") and Valerie Hunt, from UCLA, on the "Science of the Human Vibrations of Consciousness." I discovered that atoms and molecules have their own rate of vibration or frequency. Our thoughts are patterns of vibration. Our cells communicate through vibration and react to our thoughts and feelings. As I became aware of this information, I began to view my world as the energy of vibration. My perspective of life and this world completely changed. I now had tools to help me identify my own psychological constrictions stemming from negative beliefs I held about myself. I found the relationship between illness and our mental attitude so fascinating that I studied to become a naturopath and wrote a dissertation

The Geometry of Number

on Psycho-Neuro-Endocrine-Immunology (PNEI). I ended a twenty-year corporate career and haven't looked back.

When I think about how I felt when I was at my lowest point in life, on the furthest outskirts of my inner mandala, I am reminded of *Melencolia I*, by Albrecht Dürer (figure 10).

Fig. 10. *Melencolia I*, by Albrecht Dürer

Fortunately, every malady has an antidote. Dürer provided an important clue, but one has to look hard into the background. Dürer scattered alchemical symbolism (of transformation) throughout the etching, and discretely placed a magic square (figure 11) below a bell, next to time (hourglass) and a scale (Egyptian heart balance motif).

Fig. 11. Dürer's magic square, detail from *Melencolia I*

This is known as a 'magic square' because the numbers along the columns, rows, and diagonal all add up to 34. The number 34 is important because 3 represents the Tetrahedron as well as the Trinity. The number 4 is the Quaternio, or the merging into unity as we will explore later in this chapter. There is still yet another way to interpret this 'magic square.' If we remember that number holds the key to wholeness and union, and this is symbolically represented by the merging or harmony of the two opposing triangles, we have a clue to what I think Dürer was up to. Simply connect the dots. Connecting the numbers produces two intersecting triangles, an alchemical reference to the Hermetic statement, "as above, so below" (figure 12).

Fig. 12. Dürer's Star-Tetrahedron

The Geometry of Number

My life's passion is art. I consider myself a painter, to be more precise. So naturally, I was inspired to paint the Star-Tetrahedron Mandala. It is not as easy as it looks. One needs a compass, a protractor, and a ruler. Nevertheless, I was determined. Creating a Star-Tetrahedron Mandala becomes a meditation in itself. It requires lots of concentration. Because there is something archetypal about it, the exercise seems to activate latent brain centers. It is as though you are drawing the blueprint for matter as well as for the entire solar system if not Universe. The starting point is where six closest packed circles circumscribe around a seventh circle (the magic seventh heaven?):

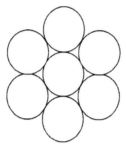

Connecting the centers of the outer circles creates the fundamental hexagon, which reveals the twin triangles when the centers are all connected. What also emerges is the pattern known as Metatron's Cube (figure 13).

Little is known about the origin of Metatron's Cube or the name Metatron. The most prevalent thinking places Metatron as the Prince (or Angel) of the Presence, as Michael the archangel, or as the transformation of Enoch after his ascent into heaven.[63] [64] [65] What does emerge is a sense of personal

63 "Metatron." Encyclopædia Britannica. Encyclopædia Britannica Online, Retrieved 11 Nov. 2011

64 "Enoch walked with God; then he was no more, because God took him away." [Genesis 5:24]

65 "...the person of Enoch, who after a lifetime of piety, was raised, according to legend, to the rank of first of the angels or literally: prince of the divine face, or

Scalar Heart Connection™

transformation. In the text, *3 Enoch*, we find, "This Enoch, whose flesh was turned to flame, his veins to fire, his eyelashes to flashes of lightning, his eye-balls to flaming torches, and whom God placed on a throne next to the throne of glory, received after this heavenly transformation the name Metatron."[66] This is similar to God adding a letter (h) from His name to Abram's and he became Abra*h*am to designate his spiritual transformation.[67] This concept is further highlighted by the curious notion that Metatron may have been God's mediator as the angel who prevented Abraham from sacrificing Isaac in the Bible story. In *Exodus*, Metatron is the angel that leads the Israelites to the Promised Land, of whom God says, "My name is in him" (vibration).[68]

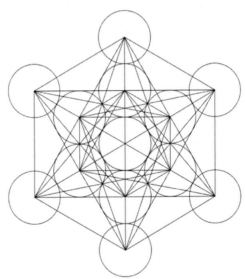

Fig. 13. Metatron's Cube.

divine presence. "God took me . . . to the heights of the seventh heaven." [Extract of 3 Enoch.] Gershom G. Scholem, Major Trends in Jewish Mysticism (Schocken, 1995) p. 67.
66 Scholem G, *Major Trends in Jewish Mysticism* (Schocken, 1995) p. 67. [Extract of 3 Enoch.]
67 *Genesis* 17:1-19
68 *Exodus* 23:21

The Geometry of Number

The essential conclusion for me is that Metatron's Cube holds the key to understanding the mystery of number. Metatron's Cube is a symbol and a tool for personal transformation. According to Abulafian Kabbalists, the proper method of gazing at Metatron's Cube leads to the image called 'Throne of Glory,' located at the heart.[69] In other words, gazing into the 'Throne of Glory' means to listen deeply with the ear within the chamber of our heart so we can connect to the Infinite. In the Kabbalah tradition, the heart can realize its nature as the mediator between the power and beauty inherent in both the finite and the Infinite.[70]

Metatron's Cube contains many geometric symbols for the unity of the finite with the Infinite. One of my favorites is the "squaring the circle."

69 Epstein P, *Kabbalah: The Way of the Jewish Mystic*, (Barnes & Noble, 1998), p. 93-94

70 Leet L, *The Secret Doctrine of the Kabbalah*, (Inner Traditions, 1999), p. 113

Metatron's Geometry of Transformation

Just remain at the center of the circle
and let all things take their course.

~ Lao Tzu

The unity and harmony between the finite and the Infinite was symbolized by a geometric puzzle posed by the
Delphic Oracle. The puzzle is known as the "squaring of the
circle." Blaming the Greek Oracle is another way of saying no
one knows where it originated. The alchemists used the symbol of the square or quaternio to represent the four elements
and the four directions; the world of the physical. In alchemical terms, the square represents the four transformational
stages. The four stages aim to distill the duality of our nature into a unity or wholeness. This is the battle of our Higher
Self versus our lower self. Moreover, the opposing four elements provide an ideal metaphor for this process of uniting
the incompatible forces of nature. Since the ultimate goal is
a unity or wholeness, the circle represents the achievement
of the goal. Jung explains that the squaring of the circle is an
alchemical symbol representing the chaotic unity of the four
elements (the physical body – the square) and then combines
them again into a higher unity (circle).[71]

In the diagram below, the perimeter of the four sides
of the square is equal to the circumference of the circle. The
symbol reveals how wholeness is contained in duality:

---

71 Jung C G, *Psychology and Alchemy*, Bollingen Series XX, (Princeton University Press, 1977), par. 165

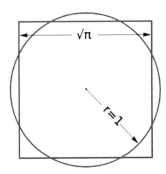

There is just one small problem with this puzzle. The geometry is impossible to construct in a finite number of steps using a compass and straightedge. The perimeter of the square presents us with four rational sides, which can be measured and calculated. The circumference of the circle eludes us with pi (π) and its never-ending decimal:

$$3.14159265358979323846\ldots$$

I don't believe this is meant as a discouragement. Rather, the symbol points to Infinity, which is the answer to the riddle. The riddle symbolizes our quest for life's answers through rational thought instead of the heart's infinity of knowing. Infinity is what quantum theorists try desperately to normalize out of their equations. It hides in the square root of 2. Infinity always leads back to itself. It is the road map to the birthplace of number.

Metatron's Cube provides an approximation of the solution. To find it, one has to actually do some work, which turns out to be the whole purpose of Metatron's Cube. First draw a circle around the six inner spheres. Then, draw a square around this circle:

Metatron's Geometry of Transformation

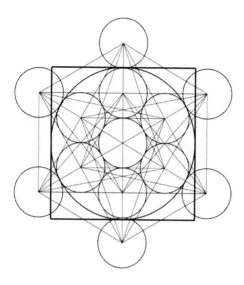

This is close, but the perimeter of the square is far from being equivalent to the circumference of the circle. The magic happens when you draw a circle through the centers of the outer circles (figure 14).

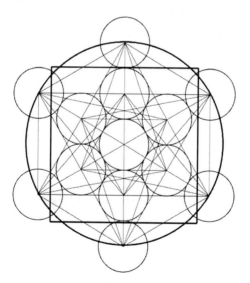

Fig. 14. Squaring the Circle with Metatron's Cube

Scalar Heart Connection™

The squaring of the circle using Metatron's Cube re-veals the inner harmony of the Earth-Moon relationship (figure 15).[72]

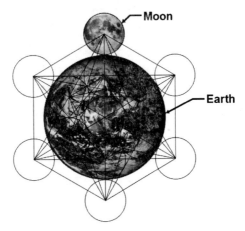

Fig. 15. The ratio of the Earth to the Moon fits almost exactly inside Metatron's Cube.

When looking closely at the numbers, we find that the radius of Earth is 3,960 miles and the Moon's radius is 1,080 miles. Their combined radii is 5,040 miles, which also equals 1 x 2 x 3 x 4 x 5 x 6 x 7 and also 7 x 8 x 9 x 10.[73] If the radius of Earth is 3,960 miles then the diameter is 7,920 miles. If you were to draw a square around Earth, the perimeter of the square would be 7,920 x 4 or 31,680 miles. The circumference of the Earth and the Moon combined is 5,040 multiplied by 2 (to arrive at the combined diameters) and then multiplied by pi (3.14159265…) or 31,667 miles. This is a difference of a mere 13 miles (13 is the number of full Moons in a year. It is also the number of spheres contained in Metatron's Cube).

72 Schneider M, *A Beginner's Guide to Constructing the Universe*, (Harper Perennial, 1995), p. 214
73 Schneider M, *A Beginner's Guide to Constructing the Universe*, (Harper Perennial, 1995), p. 214-215

Metatron's Geometry of Transformation

This means that the symbol of unity with the Infinite, the 'squaring of the circle,' is embedded in the relationship between the Moon and the Earth, which is a ratio of 3:11 (1080:3960). This ratio of 3:11 is 27.3 percent.[74] The Moon orbits the Earth every 27.3 days. Coincidentally, the average rotation period of a sunspot around the Sun is also 27.3 days.[75] It is also the average menstrual cycle.

The combined radius of the Moon and the Earth of 5,040 miles is the number that Michael Schneider (*A Beginner's Guide to Constructing the Universe*) points out is the number Plato reveals as the ideal population of human communities in *Laws*.[76] Perhaps that is a coincidence.[77] However, John Martineau points out in his book, *A Little Book of Coincidence*, that the ancients hid this relationship in the definition of the mile. There are 5,280 feet in a mile. The combined Earth and Moon circumference of 31,680 miles divides by 5,280 miles exactly 6 times. Six is the number of vertices or outer spheres in our 2-D Metatron's Cube.

Many more relationships are coincidental in our solar system. For example, the diameter of the Moon is precisely the size of the diameter of the Sun from our Earthly perspective, which is the reason a lunar eclipse exactly blocks our view of the Sun. The relationship between the Sun and the Moon relates to the alchemical notion of their celestial marriage as a symbol of ultimate Unity (coniunctio oppositorum):

---

74 Martineau J, *A Little Book of Coincidence*, (Walker & Company, 2002), p. 30
75 NASA, science.nasa.gov, (http://science.nasa.gov/science-news/science-at-nasa/2002/18jan_solarback) Retrieved 17 Nov. 2011
76 Plato, *Laws V*, 737 e
77 For more information on the Greek unit of measure related to the circumference of the Earth, see *The Acropolis Width and Ancient Geodesy*, by Nicholas Kollerstrom, The International Journal of Metrology, Fall 2005, p. 38-41 (www.dioi.org/kn/stade.pdf) Retrieved 22 Nov 2011

Scalar Heart Connection™

Total Lunar Eclipse - June 15, 2011.

When we divide the combined radii of the Earth and Moon of 5,040 by the integers 2 thru 12, the result is always a whole number, except when dividing by 11. In that case, we get the number 458.181818…ad infinitum. When we reduce 458 to what is termed the Pythagorean skein we get 4 + 5 + 8 or 17, which reduces further to 1 + 7 = 8.[78] By coincidence, NASA discovered the sun has a heartbeat of one beat every 15 or so months, which is roughly 458 days.[79] 11 is also the number of years between peak solar flare eruptions. 11 years is 132 months. That means there are 8.8 solar flare peaks per every sun heartbeat (132 divided by 15). We are going to discover later the vast significance of the number 8.

I was amazed when I first encountered all these numbers and began to see how they related to Metatron's Cube. The number 3,960 as the radius of Earth stands out because that number is equal to 11 x 360, which we just saw incorpo-

---

78 The Pythagorean skein is basically a way of transforming written language into a mathematical code. This allowed Pythagoras to convey ancient secrets in an encrypted manner that would keep the power of his mysterious knowledge out of the hands of people who would use it for destructive and coercive purposes.

79 NASA, science.nasa.gov. (http://science.nasa.gov/science-news/science-at-nasa/2000/ast03apr_1m/) Retrieved 17 Nov 2011

Metatron's Geometry of Transformation

rates the Sun's heartbeat related to 11 and 360 is the number of degrees in a circle, the symbol of unity. The only reason the Earth's radius is 3,960 miles is because of the unit measure of 5,280 feet per mile. My early saxophone playing years never got me a gig at Carnegie Hall, but I did learn enough to notice that 5,280:3,960 is 4:3 – a musical fourth. That made me think Metatron's Cube is also musical. It turns out that 6,600 is the hypotenuse of a triangle whose sides are 5,280 and 3,960 (figure 16.). The number 660 is a harmonic of time (60 seconds times 11). The number 6,600 is also a harmonic of the Sun (11 x 600).

When we create triangles by using the numbers 3,960 and 5,040 as the sides of one and 3,960 and 5,280 as the other, we discover they are almost identical in the big picture of the Cosmos (figure 16):

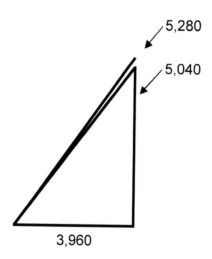

Fig. 16 Right triangles from sides 5,280 and 5,040 are almost identical.

The triangle whose sides are 3,960 and 5,040 matches the geometry of the Earth and Moon (figure 17):

Scalar Heart Connection™

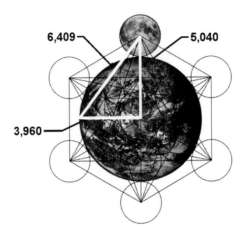

Fig. 17. The sides of a triangle whose lengths are 3,960, 5,040, and 6,409 fit inside the Earth/Moon geometry.

The triangle whose sides are 3,960, 5,280, and 6,600 almost exactly match both the geometry of Metatron's Cube and the Great Pyramid of Giza (figure 18):

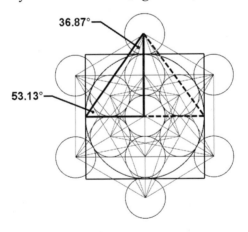

Fig. 18. The musical fourth of 5,280:3,960 creates a triangle corresponding to the Earth:Moon relationship, matching the geometry of Metatron's Cube and the Great Pyramid of Giza.

Metatron's Geometry of Transformation

It seems Leonardo da Vinci was also aware of this relationship (figure 19).

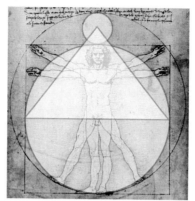

Fig. 19. The Vitruvian Man is a world-renowned drawing created by Leonardo da Vinci.

The Great Pyramid of Giza was originally about 481 feet in height and the sides measure about 755 feet in length at the base.[80] If we cut the base length in half we get 377.5. We now have a triangle whose hypotenuse calculates to be 611.45 feet with angles roughly at 90° 52° 38°. Recall the pyramid triangle in Metatron's Cube is 90° 53° 37°.

80 Hancock G. and Bauval R., *The Message of the Sphinx*, (Three River Press, 1997), p. 37

In order to construct Metatron's Cube out of musical tones or frequencies I would need more notes related to other angles. I am, however, encouraged enough to continue my search for frequencies related to health, well-being, and Unity. My search took me to Germany in 1999, where I had the great good fortune to meet physicist Fritz-Albert Popp.

Quantum Healing Codes™

The whole thing is a number.
~ Pythagoras

In the late 1970's, Fritz-Albert Popp used highly sensitive light-measuring equipment to monitor the light emitted by living cells. He confirmed that living cells emit small bursts of light as well as absorb light.[81] He further discovered that a healthy cell radiates coherent light, while a diseased cell radiates chaotic light. Popp essentially proved what other researchers described in the 1950s: that biological systems emit bio-photons in the ultra violet to the visible range of the electromagnetic spectrum.[82] Researchers have detected bio-photons in different organs and determined that photons act as regulators of physiological processes.[83] By the end of the 1970s, physicians in Germany were coming up with specific frequencies related to physiological functions.

I continued to study bioresonance in Germany. Bioresonance utilizes the body's own oscillations to help restore healthy physiological regulation. I mentored with naturopathic doctor Martin Keymer, whom at that time was also the President of the Institute of Regulative Medicine in Munich. Keymer taught me the principles of cellular regulation from a frequency perspective combined with the functionality of

81 Chang J J, Fisch J, Popp FA, *Biophotons*, (Kluwer Academic Publishers; Dordrecht, 1998)
82 Mae-Wan Ho, Fritz Albert Popp, Ulrich Warnke (editors), *Bioelectrodynamics and Biocommunication*, (World Scientific Publishing Co., 1994), p. 270
83 Ibid., p.272 (276-277)

Chinese medicine theories. Later, I studied the work of Dr. Peter Guy Manners, a British osteopath, who also collaborated with Jenny in the research of healing effects of certain sound vibrations. He developed hundreds of frequency combinations targeting various health conditions. All my studies brought me to the realization that Popp was correct when he demonstrated that healthy cells radiate 'coherent' light. What bioresonance therapists, cymatic therapists, and other vibratory modalities, including homeopathy, are ultimately trying to accomplish is the restoration of coherent resonance.

Popp's research proved that toxins and other negative environmental influences disrupt and can ultimately overwhelm the fine regulatory oscillations in the body. He said healthy cells prefer constructive wave interference patterns, which provide a powerful communication system.[84] Cells within coherent and constructive interference patterns achieve equilibrium with the chaotic frequency patterns from the outside environment. This constant interaction is life at the level of the cell. At the conscious level, our inner equilibrium is constantly challenged by outside, and often chaotic, stimuli. That is life at the level of being human. Popp concluded that tumor cells have lost the ability to maintain coherence and are no longer able to communicate.[85] That suggests that once we allow the outside chaos to overwhelm our inner sanctity and harmony, we also lose our sacred coherence and life feels difficult and joyless. I heard Lipton present similar conclusions from his research at one of his seminars. Lipton has made Popp's discoveries mainstream by explaining how "the active control of the cell is mediated by environmental signals."[86] Lipton's message is also about maintaining coherence.

84 F. A. Popp et al., Recent Advances in Biophoton Research and its Applications, eds. F. A. Popp et al., (World Scientific, Singapore, 1992)
85 Ibid.
86 Lipton B, *The Biology of Belief Course Book*, 2003, p.48

Quantum Healing Codes™

When I studied Resonance Repatterning® with founder Chloe Faith Wordsworth, I came to realize that our thoughts and emotions also have vibratory frequencies that lead to greater cellular coherence or less coherence. According to Chloe, "Coherence involves being connected; it holds things and people together; it allows for cohesiveness, consistency, integration, harmony, and unity. Our level of coherence determines the level of our health; on it depends the harmony of our relationships as well as the success and pleasure we receive from our life and work. A higher level of coherence is the place of choice: it enables us to choose how to respond to life circumstances and people. We are aware that we can react and move to a lower level of vibratory frequency into less-coherence, or we can respond in such a way that we move to a higher level of vibratory frequency, into more coherence, understanding and love."[87] It is our reaction, our response, as Lipton points out, that determines if our cells respond in an expansion mode or retract defensively. He says if we can change our perception, our "beliefs" about our environment, our physical existence on Earth, we should be able to change our lives.[88]

When we feel we never have enough money, energy, power, or time we lose coherence. That is what happened to me when I needed to see Kam Yuen. I was reacting to life with anxiety, worry, anger, and fear. My cells reacted by contracting defensively based on their 'perception' that our collective self was threatened. My new understanding that we are pulsing fields of frequency vibrations opened me to the possibility of change. All my thoughts, feelings and problems are frequencies, and frequencies can shift into phase with what is coherent. We can shift frequencies with our conscious awareness. It is a question of intention. It is a question of changing what we believe. It is a matter of changing what we think about. It is a

---

87 Wordsworth, C F, *Identifying Less-Coherent Patterns*, (Wordsworth Productions, March 2000 edition)
88 Lipton B, *The Biology of Belief Course Book*, 2003, p.48

matter of changing the habit of how we think. Sometimes, we need a little help in changing our vibration. Sometimes, listening to a tuning fork or other musical vibration is enough to re-form the wave patterns of our attitudes into coherent resonance with our positive intentions. This allows our intention, what we resonate with, to couple with the resonance of what we want. The issue is how to choose which tuning fork or to know what specific frequency to use. This question caused me to continue my search for frequency codes.

I like to believe that when I put a question out to Universe, Universe answers. I only need to be patient and keep my eyes and ears open. I was walking down the aisle of a bookstore and the title *Healing Codes* jumped out at me. Within the first several pages was a tribute by Dr. Sir Peter Guy Manners, so I knew I found my answer. *Healing Codes for the Biological Apocalypse* presents the discovery of codes or frequencies found in the Bible's Book of Numbers by naturopathic doctor Joseph Puleo (a.k.a. Dr. Barber). There is a repetition in chapter 7, beginning with verse 12, of items offered in sacrifice on specific days. Converting the verse number corresponding to the change of days into its Pythagorean skein reveals a pattern of 3s, 9s, and 6s. Recall that 396 is related to the radius of the Earth in miles. Puleo found similar patterns in *Psalm* versus 120 through 134. The result was a series of frequencies he believes are the notes in the secret Gregorian musical Sofleggio (scale)[89] used in the missing Hymn for John the Baptist. The frequencies appear in the table below:

396	417	**528**	639	741	852
= 9	= 3	= 6	= 9	= 3	= 6

The Secret tone scale that vibrates at the exact frequencies required to transform spirit to matter or matter to spirit, according to Joseph Puleo.

---

[89] "Solfeggio" - The French or Italian system in which the sol-fa syllables are used to correspond to the notes of the scale of C major.

Quantum Healing Codes™

I was ecstatic to find both 396 and 528 within these codes. Recall 528 is related to the definition of a mile. I quickly put these numbers to a spreadsheet and discovered that the Pythagorean skein of 3 9 6 continues up through the harmonics of each note. For example, the first note of 396 reduces to 9 all the way up its harmonics:

	Frequency	Pythagorean Skein
	3168	3+1+6+8=18=1+8=**9**
	2772	2+7+7+2=18=1+8=**9**
HARMONICS	2376	2+3+7+6=18=1+8=**9**
	1980	1+9+8+0=18=1+8=**9**
	1584	1+5+8+4=18=1+8=**9**
	1188	1+1+8+8=18=1+8=**9**
	792	7+9+2=18=1+8=**9**
	396	3+9+6=18=1+8=**9**

The harmonics of any note refers to the sequence of vibrations that become excited, or vibrate sympathetically, when that note is played. Early church singers noticed that when they sang a chant in a high-vaulted church, they could hear a higher note above the base melody. This higher note was the fifth note above the first octave. This phenomenon gave rise to the use of chords in later arrangements.

There is actually a whole series of notes that resonate in harmony with the fundamental note because they are all mathematical multiples of the frequency of the fundamental note. For example, the first note of the harmonic series is the first octave note, which is twice the frequency of the fundamental note. In the example of the frequency 396, the first octave note would be the frequency of 792 (396 + 396). Adding

Scalar Heart Connection™

396 to each subsequent harmonic note going up the scale produces a series of notes as follows:

	Multiple of Fundamental	Musical Interval	Frequency
	(ad. Inf.)		
HARMONICS	X8	Octave	3168
	X7	Minor seventh	2772
	X6	Octave	2376
	X5	Major 3rd	1980
	X4	Octave	1584
	X3	Perfect 5th	1188
	X2	Octave	792
		Fund. Note	**396**

The pattern of 3 6 9 is consistent with the harmonics of each of the six fundamental notes:

Musical Interval	Harmonic Frequency and Pythagorean Skein													
(ad. Inf.)														
Octave	3168	9	3336	6	4224	3	5112	9	5928	6	6816	3		
Minor 7th	2772	9	2919	3	3696	6	4473	9	5187	3	5964	6		
Perfect 5th	2376	9	2502	9	3168	9	3834	9	4446	9	5112	9		
Major 3rd	1980	9	2085	6	2640	3	3195	9	3705	6	4260	3		
Octave	1584	9	1668	3	2112	6	2556	9	2964	3	3408	6		
Perfect 5th	1188	9	1251	9	1584	9	1917	9	2223	9	2556	9		
Octave	792	9	834	6	1056	3	1278	9	1482	6	1704	3		
Fund. Note	396	9	417	3	528	6	639	9	741	3	852	6		

Quantum Healing Codes™

Unlike the equal-tempered scale in use today, some of the harmonics in the Solfeggio Scale are exactly equal to the harmonics in other fundamental notes:

Musical Interval	Harmonic Equivalents Across the Solfeggio Scale					
(ad. Inf.)						
Octave	3168	3336	4224	5112	5928	6816
Minor 7th	2772	2919	3696	4473	5187	5964
Perfect 5th	2376	2502	3168	3834	4446	5112
Major 3rd	1980	2085	2640	3195	3705	4260
Octave	1584	1668	2112	2556	2964	3408
Perfect 5th	1188	1251	1584	1917	2223	2556
Octave	792	834	1056	1278	1482	1704
Fund. Note	**396**	**417**	**528**	**639**	**741**	**852**

The complete set of harmonics, including the fundamental note, is known as "Nature's Chord" since it is present, whether audible or not, in all things. Most of the harmonics are too high to be heard by the human ear. The ones that can be heard are known as overtones and are responsible for giving musical instruments their timbre, or sound characteristics.

Note that the frequency 396 cps is in Golden Mean proportion to 639 cps as is 528 cps to 852 cps. The Golden Mean is the dividing point in any line where the smaller segment is in the same proportion to the larger segment as the larger segment is to the whole line. We will recall that the Golden Mean occurs more precisely at 1.618. 639 into 396 is equal to 1.614. 852 into 528 is also equal to 1.614.

It often happens that the area of frequency stagnation, stress or interference in the body is not the fundamental note but one of the harmonics above the fundamental note. Since the sound of the fundamental note also evokes a response from all of the harmonics, we can impact or resonate the higher notes by playing only the fundamental note. This is especially helpful when we do not have the technological means to play notes that are in the higher, inaudible range. According to Hans Kayser, a German scientist, the whole number ratios of musical harmonics correspond to an underlying framework existing in chemistry, physics, astronomy, architecture, and botany, as well as in the relationships expressed in the periodic table of elements and the formation of matter.[90]

When we examine the harmonics of the fundamental notes 396 and 528, we discover the relationships embedded in Metatron's Cube that arise from the Earth, Moon, Sun relationships (figure 20).

Harmonics of the Solfeggio Scale

6336	6672	8448	10224	11856	13632
5940	6255 → 7920		9585	1115	12780
Earth diameter — 5544	5838	7392	8946	10374	11928
The mile in feet 5148	5421	6864	8307	9633	11076
4752	5004	6336	7668	8892	10224
Earth 4356	4587	5808	7029	8151	9372
radius 3960	4170 → 5280		6390	7410	8520
3564	3753	4752	5751	6669	7668
Earth + Moon 3168	3336	4224	5112	5928	6816
circumference 2772	2919	3696	4473	5187	5964
2376	2502 → 3168		3834	4446	5112
1980	2085	2640	3195	3705	4260
1584	1668	2112	2556	2964	3408
1188	1251	1584	1917	2223	2556
792	834	1056	1278	1482	1704
396	**417**	**528**	**639**	**741**	**852**

Fig. 20. The numbers of the Solar System are harmonics of the Solfeggio Scale.

---

90 Goldman J, *Healing Sounds-The Power of Harmonics*, (Element, 1994)

Quantum Healing Codes™

The table below (figure 21) reveals the harmonics that create the Pyramid Triangle found in Metatron's Cube (from figure 17 earlier).

Harmonics of the Solfeggio Scale

The hypotenuse (actual - 6600)

Earth radius

The mile in feet

396	417	528	639	741	852
6336	6672	8448	10224	11856	13632
5940	6255	7920	9585	1115	12780
5544	5838	7392	8946	10374	11928
5148	5421	6864	8307	9633	11076
4752	5004	6336	7668	8892	10224
4356	4587	5808	7029	8151	9372
3960	4170	5280	6390	7410	8520
3564	3753	4752	5751	6669	7668
3168	3336	4224	5112	5928	6816
2772	2919	3696	4473	5187	5964
2376	2502	3168	3834	4446	5112
1980	2085	2640	3195	3705	4260
1584	1668	2112	2556	2964	3408
1188	1251	1584	1917	2223	2556
792	834	1056	1278	1482	1704
396	417	528	639	741	852

Fig. 21. The sides that make up the Pyramid Triangle in figure 11.

Connecting specific harmonics produces an infinite number of triangles:

Triangulations within the Harmonics

3960	4170	5280	6390	7410	8520
3564	3753	4752	5751	6669	7668
3168	3336	4224	5112	5928	6816
2772	2919	3696	4473	5187	5964
2376	2502	3168	3834	4446	5112
1980	2085	2640	3195	3705	4260
1584	1668	2112	2556	2964	3408
1188	1251	1584	1917	2223	2556
792	834	1056	1278	1482	1704
396	417	528	639	741	852

Scalar Heart Connection™

The triangles created by the frequencies of the harmonics have the following dimensions and angle measurements:

Trngl.	Freq. side a	Freq. side b	Freq. side c	Actual Hypot. side c	Angle (b,c)	Angle (a,c)	Side Ratio (c:a)	Metatron Side Ratio	Golden Mean (1.618)
	5112	6816	8520	8520	36.87	53.13	1.666	1.663	Yes
	3834	5112	6390	6390	36.87	53.13	1.666	1.663	Yes
	2556	3408	4260	4260	36.87	53.13	1.666	1.663	Yes
	1917	2556	3195	3195	36.87	53.13	1.666	1.663	Yes
	2502	4446	5112	5101.7	29.37	60.63	2.039	1.997	--
C	1251	2223	2556	2550.8	29.37	60.63	2.039	1.997	--
	3168	4224	5280	5280	36.87	53.13	1.666	1.663	Yes
	2376	3168	3960	3960	36.87	53.13	1.666	1.663	Yes
B	1980	3195	3753	3758.8	31.79	58.21	1.898	2.0	--
	1584	2112	2640	2640	36.87	53.13	1.666	1.663	Yes
A	1188	1584	1980	1980	36.87	53.13	1.666	1.663	Yes

Triangle A fits the shape of the Great Pyramid within 99.8% as we saw earlier. Triangle B is about 95% accurate, and Triangle C is 98% true to form. These are extremely close considering the angles have to match as well as the relative lengths of the sides. This leaves little doubt that the Solfeggio Scale encodes the geometry of Metatron's Cube, including the relationship between the Earth and the Moon:

Quantum Healing Codes™

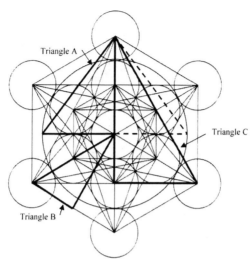

The frequency 528 stands out because its harmonics contain both the Earth's diameter (7920) and the combined circumference of Earth and Moon (3168) – related to the symbol of unity with the Infinite, 'the squaring of the circle.' The Sun is a huge photon generator. From Popp's bio-photon research, we found that our cells receive, store, and emit photons within the visual light spectrum. When we examine the light spectrum, the number 528 pops out (figure 22).

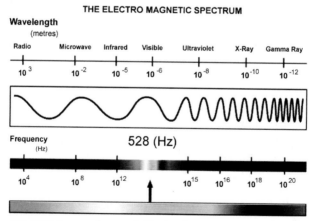

Fig. 22. 528 in terahertz falls in the middle of the visible light spectrum.

The frequency 528 is in the middle of the visible light spectrum, which is the color green. We could say it is at the heart of the light spectrum. The average human heart beats 72 times per minute. 72 times 11 equals 792, corresponding to the diameter of Earth, which we know is a harmonic of 528. Suddenly, we start to think that the human heart beats in synch with the cycles of the Sun (11 years between peak solar flare cycles). When we divide 528 by 72 we arrive at 7.333. . . (ad infinitum). I throw in the ad infinitum to remind myself that it points to Infinite. 7.333 Hz is in the range of theta brainwaves. Our brain produces frequency oscillations over its neuron networks that are measurable with scalp EEG.[91] Theta waves are in the range of cerebral rhythmic activity between 5 and 8 Hz, which encompasses our calculated number of 7.333. Theta is the brainwave state of creativity, intuition and insight.[92] The lowest range of theta frequencies is related to deep meditation and healing potential.[93] These are all qualities of the heart, which makes sense because, as researchers at the Institute of HeartMath demonstrated, brain rhythms synchronize to the heart's electromagnetic pulses.[94] It is not surprising that theta waves are associated with the color green.[95]

Every day the human heart is surrounded by an atmospheric standing wave that oscillates on average at a rate of 7.86 cps. This energy resonance was first mathematically predicted by Winfried Otto Schumann in the early 1950s, although Nikola Tesla documented his observations of global electromagnetic standing waves as early as 1899.[96] Hundreds

---

91 Electroencephalography (EEG) is the recording of electrical activity along the scalp. EEG measures voltage fluctuations resulting from ionic current flows within the neurons of the brain.

92 Burnham S, *The Art of Intuition: Cultivating Your Inner Wisdom*, (Tarcher/ Penguin, 2011), p. 149-150

93 Ibid.

94 McCraty R, *The Resonant Heart*, Shift: At the Frontiers of Consciousness, Dec. 2004 / Feb 2005, p.16

95 Ibid., p. 151

96 Tesla N, (1905) "The Transmission of Electrical Energy Without Wires As

Quantum Healing Codes™

of lightning bolts strike the Earth every second creating a vibration or resonance pattern between the Earth's surface and the inner layer of the ionosphere (the earth-ionosphere cavity). These electromagnetic standing waves travel around the globe at the speed of light, circumnavigating the globe at a rate of 7.86 times per second.[97] Not surprising, the frequency of 7.8 Hz is the precise frequency of the hippocampus in all mammals, including humans.[98] Our nervous system also responds to the electromagnetic pulses of Schumann waves and their wide range of harmonics. This is why NASA builds Schumann wave generators into their manned satellites. Schumann waves have a twenty-four hour cycle as the iosphere rises at night due to the cooler temperature, reducing the pulse rate to coincide with the rhythm of our brain waves during sleep.

The Schumann resonance of 7.86 Hz sets up a kind of Earth heart rate or earthbeat that the human heart entrains to at 7.33 Hz along with our intuitive theta brain waves in the 7 - 8 Hz range. The question arises, how can I maintain equilibrium with the earthbeat that is coherent with the harmonious resonance of the heart? If these frequencies surround me, then why am I not experiencing joy and harmony? I believe the answer lies within the geometries of Metatron's Cube. Number and geometry might just prove to be helpful in determining what outside frequencies are impinging on our inner coherence. More important, with the help of the codes, we might also be able to restore coherence and equilibrium.

But, before we move on to looking into the chambers of the heart, I feel obligated to point out one more 'coincidence' within Metatron's Cube. It relates to the number 72; the fre-

---

A Means Of Furthering World Peace" *Electrical World and Engineer,* January 7: 21–24

97 Oschmann J, *Energy Medicine - The Scientific Basis,* (Churchill Livingstone, 2001), p. 185

98 O'Keefe J, Nadel L, *The Hippocampus as a Cognitive Map,* (Clarendon Press; Oxford 1974)

Scalar Heart Connection™

quency of the heart. A triangle whose base is in Golden Mean proportion to each of its sides is a Golden Triangle (figure 23).

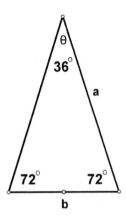

Fig. 23. A Golden Triangle. The ratio a:b is equivalent to the golden ratio.

Metatron's Cube also contains a Golden Triangle, whose angles are 71.75° or within 99.7 percent accurate (figure 24).

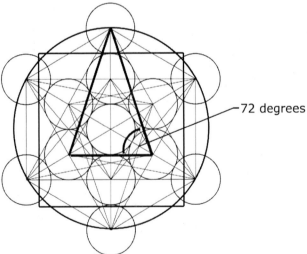

Fig 24. The Golden Triangle in Metatron's Cube contains the heart.

Quantum Healing Codes™

Metatron's Golden Triangle is close enough to remind us we are not perfect. Hence, the transformative symbol of Metatron. This concept goes back to ancient times. The image below (figure 25) is from the seventeenth century alchemical text, Scrutinium Chymicum (Scrutiny of Chemistry), by Michaelis Majeri (a.k.a. Michael Maier):

Fig. 25. Squaring of the circle to unite male and female (duality) into One.

The Golden Triangle is apparent in the above image with its 72° angles encompassing the yin and yang energies, depicted by the male and female inside the circle. In *Psychology and Alchemy*, Jung, in connection with this image, quotes from another alchemical text: "Make a round circle and you will have the philosophers' stone."[99] The number 72 is a number of the heart as is 528. The symbol of the interlaced Tetrahedrons is the symbol of the heart chakra in Eastern Indian tradition. We also saw that 528 corresponds to the color green, which is the color of the heart chakra. The interlaced Tetrahedrons below (figure 26), in Kabbalah tradition, refer to the "double heart" found in the concept of Tiferet as the energy of love and the intention to put light and love into the world.[100]

99 Jung C G, *Psychology and Alchemy*, Bollingen Series XX (Princeton University Press, 1977), p. 128
100 Dolnick B, *Enlighten Up: The Keys to Kabbalah*, (New American Library,

Scalar Heart Connection™

Fig. 26. Tiferet is the mediator and integrator of the two
inclinations of the heart.[101]
One Tetrahedron points upwards to the Heavens and the other
towards Earth.

So far, we have looked at the heart's resonance with
Earth, Moon, and Sun. But, if we look beyond our solar system, to the fixed stars, we find the heart is again in synch with
the geometry and rhythmicity of Galactic scales. The time it
takes for the fixed stars to move in relation to Earth's horizon is the Precession of the Equinoxes. It is explained by the
unusual fact that our planet, spinning like a top, has a slight
wobble, which tracks in the opposite direction of its orbital
path around the Sun (figure 27). This accounts for why the
constellations appear in reverse order of their customary zo-
diacal progression (hence, the term "precession"). The time
it takes to pass through all twelve constellations is one Great
Cycle; about 25,920 years (often rounded to 26,000 years).

2005), p. 75-76
101 Leet L, *The Secret Doctrine of the Kabbalah*, (Inner Traditions, 1999), p. 172

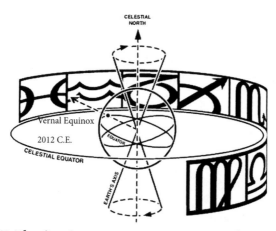

Fig. 27. The fixed stars appear to parade behind the Sun
in reverse order as seen at the Summer Equinox.
(Image courtesy of Courtney Roberts, author of
The Star of the Magi. Illustration by Michael G. Conrad)

It takes 72 years to complete one arc second of the
Great Cycle (72 x 360° = 25,920). Notice the Golden Triangle
(above) contains the angles 36° and 72°. The zodiac is divided
into 12 constellations. It takes 2,160 years for the precession to
pass through one zodiac sign or Age (also Aion or Aeon). It
just so happens that the diameter of the Moon is 2,160 miles.
Indian yogic schools hold that all living beings inhale and ex-
hale 21,600 times per day in harmony with the celestial Great
Cycle of 2,160 years per Aion.[102] Thanks to the wisdom of the
Ancients, we have a mile (5,280 feet) that gives us these fan-
tastic coincidences. The number of feet in a mile connects the
time of celestial orbits with the planetary space of their diameters and circumferences.

If we look at the time it takes the Precession to march
through two Aions, we arrive at 2,160 x 2 or the number 4,320.
The number 4,320 is famous as the number of years in an 'epoch' or 'era' in Hindu philosophy (432,000 years equals one

---

102 Campbell J, *The Inner Reaches of Outer Space*, (Perennial Library, 1988), p. 87

Yuga).[103] When we multiply this epoch by the Sun's 11-year-cycle we arrive at the number 47,520 (4,320 x 11). The number 4752 is a harmonic frequency of the heart (72 x 66). From the harmonic chart below, we find that 4752 is also an octave above the Solfeggio Scale of both 396 and 528:

Harmonics of the Solfeggio Scale

6336	6672	8448	10224	11856	13632
5940	6255	7920	9585	1115	12780
5544	5838	7392	8946	10374	11928
5148	5421	6864	8307	9633	11076
4752	5004	6336	7668	8892	10224
4356	4587	5808	7029	8151	9372
3960	4170	5280	6390	7410	8520
3564	3753	4752	5751	6669	7668
3168	3336	4224	5112	5928	6816
2772	2919	3696	4473	5187	5964
2376	2502	3168	3834	4446	5112
1980	2085	2640	3195	3705	4260
1584	1668	2112	2556	2964	3408
1188	1251	1584	1917	2223	2556
792	834	1056	1278	1482	1704
396	**417**	**528**	**639**	**741**	**852**

The number 4,320 also relates to the number of heartbeats in an hour (72 x 60 minutes). An octave above 4,320 is 8,640. There are 86,400 seconds in a day. The diameter of the Sun is 864,000 miles. Again, time and space are harmonious.

In the following chapters, we will discover the physiological connection to the numbers 60, relating to breathing, and 72, the beating of the heart. On the level of number, 72 and 60 are related to the Great Cycle of 25,920 (72 x 360) and 21,600, the number of breaths we take each day (60 x 360). The number 360 is the number of degrees in a circle, representing wholeness. The numbers 25,920 and 21,600 are in a ratio of

---

103 There are 432,000 years in the present cycle of time, the so-called Kali Yuga. See Joseph Campbell, *The Inner Reaches of Outer Space*, (Perennial Library, 1988), p. 35

Quantum Healing Codes™

6:5. This is the same ratio of 72:60, which is a musical minor third. When we apply this ratio to the Golden Mean squared (phi squared or 2.618) we arrive at pi (π or 3.14159). In other words, the ratio 6:5 is the same as 1.2, therefore 2.618 multiplied by 1.2 is equivalent to 3.1416. This minor third musical ratio of the heart and breath mathematically unites the Divine Ratio with the circumference of a circle, the symbol of Unity and Wholeness.

The magical ratio of 72:60, our beating heart (72) and time (60 – also related to our breathing rate), relates harmonically to Earth, Moon, Sun, and Aions of time (see table below):

Harmonics of the Heartbeat and Time/Breath

Heartbeat		Time/Breath	
8640	seconds in a day (86,400) / diam. of Sun (864,000)	8640	seconds in a day (86,400) / diam. of Sun (864,000)
7920	diameter of Earth	7920	diameter of Earth
4752	Aion mult. by Sun	5280	feet in a mile
4320	heartbeats per hour	4320	heartbeats per hour
3960	radius of Earth	3960	radius of Earth
3168	Earth squared (31,680)		
2160	breaths per day (21,600) / Aion of Time / diam. of Moon	2160	breaths per day (21,600) / Aion of Time/ diam. of Moon
1440	Harmonic of the heart	1440	harmonic of the heart
1080	radius of Moon	1080	radius of Moon
		900	breaths per hour
792	diam. of Earth – 72 x 11 (Sun)	720	harmonic of the heart
		660	60 x 11 (Sun) / 72 x 66 = 4752 (a harmonic of the heart)
144	1st harmonic of the heart	120	1st harmonic of time
72		**60**	

Scalar Heart Connection™

The Quantum Healing Codes™ also contain a minor third chord in the ratio of 6:5. I call this the "Open Heart Chord." It is a combination of the notes 639 and 528, as well as the notes 396 and 852. The codes 639 and 528 are in ratio of 6:5. I sent an audio file of the "Open Heart Chord" to CymaScope. The people at CymaScope used this file to create a CymaGlyph utilizing the equipment similar to Jenny. The image below is the resulting CymaGlyph of the "Open Heart Chord":

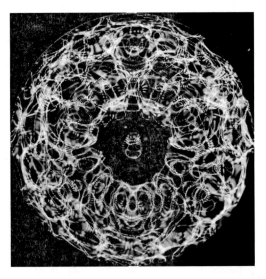

CymaGlyph of "Open Heart Chord" by CymaScope.com

This image is quite complex as well as harmonious. There are fourteen antinodes surrounding the center, creating a seven-sided figure, the Heptagon:

Quantum Healing Codes™

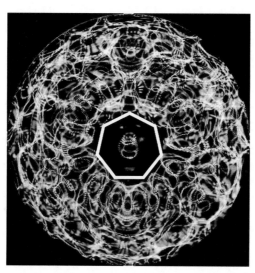

The "Open Heart Chord" with a Heptagon in the middle.

I was curious as to why the "Open Heart Chord" would result in a geometry related to the number 14. The answer came to me when I re-examined Plato's famous number 5040. Recall the numbers 3960, the Earth's radius, and 1080, the Moon's radius, add to 5040. When we divide 5040 by 360, the number of degrees in a circle (the number of wholeness), we get the number 14. The Moon waxes and wanes approximately 14 days each. The Heptagon reveals that the number 7, the number of the heart, is also harmonically connected to the planets. Note that pi, the circumference of any circle or planet, is 22/7.[104]

The relationships between the numbers pertaining to the heart and those of Earth, Moon, Sun, and Galaxy provide clues as to why Ancient civilizations believed the cosmic order is mathematically discoverable. Campbell describes that Ancient civilizations realized that society and its individual members are equal products of nature; correlating as one measure, the cycles of the celestial spheres, the cycles of time,

104 Information provided by John Stuart Reid, CymaScope.com

and the pulsations of the human heart.[105] The Ancients seem to have placed a strong emphasis on connecting the heart with the earthbeat. I found the musical rhythms of the beating heart and its relationship with the cycles of time and space to be fascinating. I began to imagine how the Ancients would have described our current situation, where our heart is no longer in harmony with the rhythms of Nature. I wondered if they had imagined a kind of double heart, one no longer connected to the earthbeat and Universe.

---

105 Campbell J, *The Inner Reaches of Outer Space*, (Perennial Library, 1988), p. 87

The Double Heart

Your vision will become clear only when you look into
your heart.
Who looks outside, dreams. Who looks inside, awakens.
~ C.G. Jung

The heart is a frequency counting system. It navigates numerically through the energy field of spacetime, capable of distinguishing between the good, the bad, and the ugly (the harmonious from the disharmonious). The heart beats to a rhythm synchronized to oscillations of our planet and phases of the Moon, which keep pace to the cycles of the sun. The heart is at the center of the perception of number. Its rhythmic beating establishes the body's rhythm and the norm against which other rhythms are counted and compared.[106] The pulsing waves of energy from the heart radiate and interact with organs, body systems, cells, and DNA. Brain rhythms synchronize to the heart's electromagnetic pulses. Our heart relays fluctuations in frequency oscillations within the energy field of Universe to mind-brain consciousness in the form of feeling. This helps explain why consciousness is aware we are thinking before we think about it. It is the basis of our heart's intuitive nature.

The esoteric identification of the heart with the deeper, intuitive understanding relates to its ability to perceive these subtle vibrations within spacetime and beyond. The Hindu sage, Vasistha, said, "When objects as well as the experiencing

---

106 Leet L, *The Secret Doctrine of the Kabbalah*, (Inner Traditions, 1999), p. 91

mind have become tranquil, consciousness alone remains."[107] It is the same consciousness that reverberates through all of us. It is the same consciousness that makes it impossible to distinguish the 'living' from the 'non-living.' This energy field of consciousness is omnipresent, omnipotent, and omniscient.

The Kabbalists had a unique term. It is the concept of the "Double Heart." The Star of David or the superimposed double triangles of the hexagon symbolize the Double Heart. The upward triangle represents the spiritual. The downward facing triangle refers to the physical. The heart knows what we are thinking. If our thought-forms are about survival, safety, reproduction, and other worldly desires, then we are activating the downward pointing triangle. This downward flow concerns itself with receiving and activates our 'gut' responses, where anger, fear, greed, and envy reside. The upward heart has the quality of an outward flow, characteristic of the heart's physical circulation.[108] The outward flow manifests as unconditional love and desires only to unite its fullness with others and the Infinite.[109]

The double heart is the perfect metaphor for the mandala symbol. Recall how the mandala represents our journey from the outer edges back to the center of wholeness and harmony with the Infinite. The 'outer edges' of the mandala is synonymous with the lower Tetrahedron where we tend to create or perceive most of our conflicts and problems in the world. Recall also the dual energy currents in the body. Maya is the Yin energy drawing us into physical creation, while Sophia is calling our Yang energy to re-unite with the Infinite. The two currents intertwine like the caduceus staff, commingling along the spine where we find vortices of energy known as chakras:

---

107 Venkatesananda S, *The Concise Yoga Vasistha*, (State University of New York Press, 1985), p. 142
108 Leet L, *The Secret Doctrine of the Kabbalah*, (Inner Traditions, 1999) , p. 174
109 Ibid.

The Double Heart

The lowest of these centers is the root chakra and is associated with elimination. It is related to the alimentary canal; everything we put into our mouths and everything that goes out the other end. I think of it as the 'elementary' canal because it is the most basic of life needs. It is the animal instinct of finding sustenance—killing something to eat. It is also concerned with having a place to sleep and warm clothing—the basics of life. Once we are fed and have the basics covered we can get on to the business of creating more beings like us; the instinct of procreation. The center of this energy is in the second chakra center located at the area of the pelvis. This is where we typically experience the force of the libido, which is the same energy; it is only a question of where it is focused. The third chakra is at the level of the solar plexus and corresponds to assertiveness, power, and control. It is the chakra of will-directed action. After we are fed and sexually satisfied then our will comes in and says, "Now what do you want?" The answer is usually 'more food and more sex.' In the animal kingdom, this question doesn't generally arise. Animals seem content with the basics. Human beings, on the other hand, seem to always want more of everything. Unfortunately, desire leads to wanting more, which can lead to territorial disputes with our neighbors. Therefore, we create conflict. Conflict is both internal, as our life energy swirls around the lower three chakra centers trying to find peace and contentment, which is not found in the lower centers, and externally in our outward attempt to acquire more things and possessions from our neighbors.

The solution, I'm convinced, lies in our ability to first become aware of the source of our desires and conflicts coming from the lower chakras and to then move into the fourth chakra, the heart – the center of compassion and connection. It is the center where the thought of 'self' is secondary to the realization that we are part of a whole: a community, a country, a planet, a universe. The true spiritual path starts at the heart chakra and leads to the throat, brow and crown chakras – the spiritual centers – after the lower three are mastered.

The evolutionary challenge for human beings lies in how we strike equilibrium with the outside frequency oscillations that bombard us each day. It is actually healthy to be challenged, similar to how our cells are in a constant state of mediating between our perceptions of what is life threatening and what is life enhancing. When we find ourselves out of balance with what we want to attract in our lives, it is generally an indication that our coherence is chaotic and breaking down due to an imbalance in one of the lower chakras.

The Chakra System

The word "chakra" has its origin in Hindu texts, derived from the Sanskrit word "cakra" meaning "wheel" or "turning." In Buddhism, it is the Pali word "cakka" in the sense of "circle." The word refers to the spiraling vortices of life force or cosmic energy found along the spinal column. These centers of bioenergetic activity are found emanating from the major nerve ganglia branching forward from the spinal column.[110] They are also associated with major endocrine glands. Each chakra has its own unique frequency vibration, harmonic pattern, specific color, and each serves as energy transformers providing sequentially stepped-down energy to various hormonal, physiological, and cellular process in the body.[111] [112]

Candace Pert, a neuroscientist and pharmacologist, discovered the opiate receptor, which is a vibrating cellular binding site for endorphins in the brain and body.[113] Her research has since expanded to include scientific research on the chakra system. She refers to the chakras as 'minibrains' or nodal points of electrical and chemical activity that receive, process, and distribute information to the rest of the body-mind system.[114] She describes the chakras as sites of neuronal plexus or networks of cells dense with neuropeptide transmitters.[115] The chakras are connected to each other and work

110 Anodea J, *Eastern Body, Western Mind : Psychology and the Chakra System as a Path to the Self*, (Celestial Arts, 1996), p.5
111 Gerber R, *Vibrational Medicine*, (Bear & Company, 1988), p.128
112 Matsumoto K, Birch S, *Extraordinary Vessels*, (Paradigm Publications, 1986), p.6
113 Pert C, *Molecules of Emotion; The Science Behind Mind-Body Medicine*, (Touchstone, 1999), p. 21-22
114 Pert C, *Your Body is Your Subconscious Mind*, (Sounds True, 2000)
115 Ibid.

together to maintain balance and govern certain subconscious decisions.[116] Likewise, she says, trauma or neglect can block one or more of the chakra nodal points and degrade the performance of the entire system.[117]

Each chakra also influences the organs and all other systems within its energy field. The chakras resonate with various aspects of the human experience from the urge and preservation of life, to life's unfolding, self-empowerment and individuation, to the capacity for unconditional love, expression, comprehension, to the longing for union with the Infinite.

The chakras are traditionally associated with the colors of the spectrum from the red of the root chakra to violet of the crown.[118]

ROOT

The first chakra is located at the base of the spine (below the tailbone, pelvic floor). It is associated with the color red and the element Earth. The energy of the root chakra carries the life force up the body as well as down the legs connecting us to the primordial energies of the Earth. It also moves to the front of the body as it spins over the sexual organs. Our life experiences are first imprinted at this primordial level where the energetic memory of childhood and ancestral emotions are held. This is the energy of instincts related to survival and self-preservation.

Disharmony in this center arises from insecurity, greed, and self-centered instinctual behaviors involving aggression, dominance, and territoriality. When this center is disharmonious, its power to fuel the other chakras diminishes.

The harmonious energy of the root chakra is about

---

116 Ibid.
117 Ibid.
118 Hunt V, et al., *A Study of Structural Integration from Neuromuscular, Energy Field, and Emotional Approaches*, Rolf Institute of Structural Integration, 1977.

The Chakra System

connection with the Earth and its inhabitants. It is about staying safe and helping others in the community feel physically secure. It is the origin of the impulse of honor, loyalty, and identification with our children.[119]

PELVIS

The second chakra is located between the navel (about 2 inches below) and the top of the pelvis. It is associated with the color orange and the water element. The pelvis chakra is the area of the womb. It is the energy of the water element, which nourishes the cells of the unborn baby. Its energy relates to survival issues on the level of procreation. As such, it focuses on sexual drive as well as the creative impulse. It is the center where imagination and creativity germinate and pour through our sense of being.[120] It is also an emotional center related to desire and sensory pleasures.

Disharmony of this center manifests through the pain of sexual conflicts, low creative drive, frustration, confusion, indecision, resistance to change, lack of spontaneity, unfulfilled yearning, a sense of incompleteness, and feelings of guilt.[121] The result can be low self-esteem, lack of confidence in one's own creativity, lack of direction, jealousy, envy, possessiveness, over-indulgence in food and / or sex (drugs, alcohol, etc.).

The harmonious energy of the pelvis chakra is playfulness, innocence, goodness, and generosity.[122] Pelvis energy is creative, has faith and trust in the big picture of life, is protective and womb-like; extending a comfort to others.

SOLAR PLEXUS

---

119 Eden D, *Energy Medicine*, (Jeremy P. Tarcher/Putnam, 1998), p.146
120 Ibid p.149
121 *Dr. Berkowsky's Six Element Paradigm Workbook*, (Joseph Ben Hil-Meyer Research, Inc., 2010), p.22
122 Eden D, *Energy Medicine*, (Jeremy P. Tarcher/Putnam, 1998), p.148

Scalar Heart Connection™

The third chakra is located at the solar plexus (pit of stomach) and is associated with the color yellow and the fire and wood elements. The solar plexus chakra is associated with physiological activities related to digestion, particularly to metabolism and the regulation/production of mitochondria energy. Hence, the solar plexus is considered as the fire center. It is also the energy that maintains our sense of identity—our personal ego. It is the center holding the energy of discrimination and assertion.[123] This center imprints our ideas of social expectations: who we want to be, who we think we are, and who we think we should be.[124] This center is almost the reverse of the second chakra: logical rather than creative, cunning instead of innocent, suspicious instead of trusting, and responsible instead of flowing.[125] This center holds the energy of the controlling parent rather than the inner child of the second center.[126]

Imbalances in this chakra manifest as a desire for power, fame, and dominance over others. One may be overly sociable and unable to enjoy one's own company. One may be easily overwhelmed by anxiety, panic, excessive worry, insecurity, low self-esteem, fear of rejection, indecisiveness, oversensitivity to criticism, self-consciousness, and/or incapable of opening to greater things in life.[127]

The harmonious energy of the solar plexus allows the second chakra's spontaneity, trust, and faith to rise and allow a more gentle, kinder self to rise to the fourth chakra of connection with nature and others, to the expression of love, and expanded states of awareness and unity with the cosmos.

---

123 Ibid., p. 152
124 Ibid.
125 Ibid., p. 153
126 Ibid.
127 *Dr. Berkowsky's Six Element Paradigm Workbook*, (Joseph Ben Hil-Meyer Research, Inc., 2010), p.23

The Chakra System

HEART

The fourth chakra, or heart chakra, is located at the center of the chest and is associated with the color green and the element air. Indigenous people have always considered thinking to come from the heart, guided more by the intuition of the heart than by the head[128] – more by feeling and love than by logic. When we are connected to the heart we are able to express love, both self-love and love towards others. The lessons of love may be the most important of all experiences on the physical plane – the lesson of unconditional love. Polishing the walls of the vessel of the heart makes it transparent and open to the highest form of spiritual love and infinite intelligence – one reason the heart is considered the seat of the soul within the body. The heart chakra sits midway between the lower three chakras, representing the physical plane, and the higher three chakras of the higher transcendent plane.

Imbalances in the fourth chakra can manifest as emotional disability, codependency, neediness, and possessiveness.

A balanced heart chakra enables one to rise above egoistic love. An open heart is forgiving of self and others and connected to the forces of peace and harmony. It allows for the development of compassion and empathy for others and is the first step towards attaining higher levels of consciousness.

THROAT

The fifth chakra is located at the area of the throat and is associated with the color cyan or sky blue. It relates to the element ether or light. The throat chakra is about communication. The energy of the lower chakras move up to the throat where it is assimilated (metabolized) and synthesized into

---

128 Jung C G, edited by Jaffe A, *Memories, Dreams, Reflections,* (Vintage Books, 1989), p.248

our unique voice and expression in the world.[129]

Imbalances in the fifth chakra manifest as not being able to speak out or not being able to be quiet. Silence is similar to the catabolic process of receiving and assimilating. Speaking is the anabolic equivalent – putting ideas together and expressing them.[130]

When the throat chakra is balanced we naturally allow time for others to speak their truth and provide time for ourselves to digest and integrate our thoughts before speaking out. This creates an open and balanced relationship between ourselves and others.

BROW

The sixth chakra is located midway between the eyebrows and is associated with the color indigo (dark blue) and the element ether or light. The brow chakra is associated with the frontal lobe of the brain, the pituitary gland, and the coordination of the left and right hemispheres of the brain. Our capacity for abstract thought in this center allows us to transcend the physical as we explore the world of symbols, theories, and meaning. The energy of this chakra allows us to transcend our ego identity and fine-tunes our extra-sensory perceptions.

Imbalances in the brow chakra manifest as preoccupations with mental constructs and fantasies that crowed out more subtle ways of knowing.[131] It manifests at its worse when its thinking turns towards jealousy, fear, greed, power and other ego-based ambitions derived from an imbalanced solar plexus chakra.[132] Disharmonies can also give rise to poor concentration, anxiety, estrangement from oneself and the

---

129 Eden D, *Energy Medicine*, (Jeremy P. Tarcher/Putnam, 1998), p.156
130 Ibid., p. 157
131 Ibid., p. 159
132 Ibid., p. 160

The Chakra System

world, cynicism, disturbed sleep and unpleasant dreams.[133]

When the brow chakra is open, we are able to perceive the true nature of things as we experience heightened awareness. It helps facilitate intuition, wisdom, understanding, knowledgeable insight, imagination and imaginative consciousness, connection to spirit, psychic powers, and a peaceful presence of being.[134]

CROWN

The seventh chakra is located at the top of the head and is associated with the color violet and the element ether and light. The crown chakra is associated with the pineal gland, the organ of light. It is associated with complete openness to divine light, oneness with the universe, and unity with the Source.

An imbalance in the crown chakra can cause one to feel deprived of sustained experiential connection to the Divine. A blocked crown chakra can lead to confusion, depression, lack of inspiration, and a sense of estrangement with self and others.

A harmonious crown chakra attunes one to the "knowledge" of meaning and deepens our awareness of our connection with others, the planet, with Infinity.

---

133 *Dr. Berkowsky's Six Element Paradigm Workbook*, (Joseph Ben Hil-Meyer Research, Inc., 2010), p.26
134 Ibid.

The Chakras and Metatron's Cube

The frequencies of the Solfeggio codes (see chapter "Quantum Healing Codes™") relate to the colors of the chakras. The chart below shows the Solfeggio frequencies stated as wavelengths in nanometer and then by frequency oscillations stated in terahertz. There is an inverse relationship between the wavelength of light, measured in nanometers, and its frequency rate. The longer the wavelength the fewer frequency oscillations it contains. The table below (figure 26) compares the color spectrum with the frequencies of the Solfeggio codes:

	Wavelength (nanometer)	Solfeggio Code wave (nm)	freg. (THz)	Chakra Correlation
Red	620-750	757(a) 719 704	396 417 426(b)	396
Orange	590-620			417
Yellow	570-590			426
Green	495-570	568	528	528
Cyan	476-495			639
Blue	450-475	469	639	741
Violet (UV)	380-450	405 352	741 852	852
(a) Infrared				
(b) Octave below 852				

Fig. 28. The Solfeggio Codes and their Chakra Correlations.

The Chakras and Metatron's Cube

It is apparent that the Solfeggio frequencies group together on the lowest side of the spectrum (infrared) and around the highest end (ultraviolet). Infrared is a long and slow vibration, one associated with the Earth element. These are low frequencies like the sounds elephants or whales make. Ultraviolet waves are short in length and contain a high frequency rate. Fritz-Albert Popp found this spectrum in biophotons involved in healthy cellular processes.

I distributed the frequencies more evenly so they would align with the traditional chakra colors. I remembered from art school that yellow is the complementary color of violet. Therefore, I felt justified in moving 426, which is the lower octave of 852 (violet) to the level of yellow – the solar plexus chakra. The complement of blue (741) is orange (417), which allowed me to place those two codes into the chakras at the pelvis and crown chakra positions respectively. I wanted to justify moving 639 to cyan because of its numeric relationship to 396, but the complement of red is green, not cyan. Then I remembered that the complements of colors in pigment are not the same as the colors found in light. The complements in pigment combine to make black or dark gray. The complements of colors in light combine to make pure white light (figure 29).

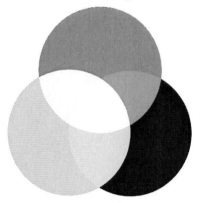

Fig. 29. The RGB model of light frequencies combines into pure white light.

We will see in a later chapter how the chakras below the heart have complements in the chakras above the heart similar to the complements found in color. When the chakras are balanced, they merge together, harmoniously, and pure white light emerges. This is metaphoric for how duality works together to reunite as One.

I could imagine how the coming together of the double heart leads to a deeper, intuitive, even spiritual experience. But, I felt that something was missing for me on a more physical level. I saw how Metatron's Cube acted like a symbol for the ultimate human journey and how it related to the chakras and their various emotional qualities. I imaged Metatron's Cube as a mandala, leading me back to its center and away from the far corners of my emotional chaos. What I was not putting together was how to access my heart's innate wisdom. I wondered what the mechanism was that allowed my heart to know the life-inhibiting emotions I carried deep within my subconscious. If I am energy, a being of energy, how can I harness that energy? That was the question I put to Universe. I only had to wait for a reply.

Scalar Waves

With realization of one's own potential
and self-confidence in one's ability,
one can build a better world.
~ Dalai Lama

In 2001, I heard Valerie Hunt speak at the annual convention of the American Naturopathic Medical Association. She is "professor emeritus" of Physiological Science at UCLA and the first person to have developed the protocols and instrumentation necessary to detect and record the body's high frequency energy fields with the spectral analysis of bioenergy patterns. At a breakout session at the ANMA conference, she described how deep breathing produces scalar waves. She had everyone present breathe deeply and imagine energy traveling up our spines as our breath excited scalar potentials through the möbius coil of our spine. She told us how we could direct scalar waves to areas of our body through our intention. I was fascinated, but I could not visualize how my spine produced scalar waves.

I returned from the conference and quickly ordered a copy of her book, *Infinite Mind: Science of the Human Vibrations of Consciousness*. I was hoping to find a detailed explanation to satisfy my curious mind. A few months prior, I had met James Oschman at a Holographic Repatterning Association convention. Oschman lectured on his new book, *Energy Medicine, the Scientific Basis*. In later correspondence with James, I came to learn more about how scalar waves are produced.

When two waves come together and they are in phase

Scalar Heart Connection™

with each other there is an additive effect; they combine into a larger wave. This is termed 'constructive interference.' When two waves come together that are out of phase with each other, they can cancel out or destroy each other. This is 'destructive interference' as seen in figure 30.[135]

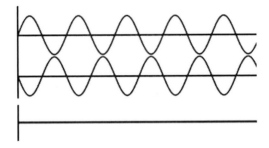

Fig. 30. Destructive interference.

In *Energy Medicine, the Scientific Basis*, Oschman explains that in the case of cancelled or destroyed waves, the result is not exactly an annihilation of magnetic fields but a transformation into an energy field or a standing wave that can no longer be measured in terms of amplitude or current flow. Yet, its energy remains in what came to be called 'potential waves.' Oschman points out that for a long time these potential waves were not thought to exist except as mathematical abstractions.[136] A paper co-authored in 1959 by Yakir Aharonov and David Bohm predicted that scalar waves actually exist. Later experiments confirmed their prediction in what is called the Aharonov-Bohm effect.

Perhaps the example of two equal teams at tug of war will help illustrate the concept of scalar potential. As long as the teams are pulling with equal strength there will be tre-

135 Oschman J, *Energy Medicine; the Scientific Basis*, (Churchill Livingston, 2001), p. 204
136 Ibid., p. 203

mendous energy or force exerted on the rope, but at the center of the rope one could say that at this zero point there is no net energy because the opposite forces being exerted by the equal tug-of-war teams have cancelled out the energy in the middle. The middle point of the rope appears not to be moving or to possess energy. What we have, in effect, is the potential for energy as soon as the opposing teams come out of balance and one team dominates. Therefore, when two or more electric or magnetic fields sum to zero, there is still a stressed or locked-in potential of energy. As long as the energy is balanced there is no measurable energy, even when the fields that are creating the 'zero-point' or 'vacuum' possess infinitely vast amounts of energy.

In this case, one must consider that scalar waves may be the 'real' energy source, while the fields are only the measurable effects. What we may think of as an 'empty' vacuum, known as the quantum vacuum, is actually 'packed full' of potential, which sums to zero in a stable state, giving us the illusion that there is 'nothing there.' This is known as the virtual state of electrostatic scalar potential, a scalar value being one characterized by magnitude only, i.e., potential without manifestation (the quintessential human being).

The unexpressed energy potential of the two teams at tug-of-war can be seen as being interconnected to all of the players simultaneously. A change in force in one of the players will affect the outcome for both teams. Oschman points out that scalar potential propagates instantaneously everywhere in space, undiminished by distance.[137] He suggests a relationship between scalar waves and subtle interactions at a distance, including the phenomena of synchronicity and healing at a distance.[138] And, we have just come full circle back to the concept of 'space resonance' where all matter is connected by scalar waves propagating in the medium of space.

137 Ibid., p. 206
138 Ibid., p. 207

We are all connected to each other in the same scalar field. We are connected to the energy source that makes up Universe (we are all holding on to the rope). We are totally inter-dependent. Our bodies, our brains, and our consciousness are inextricably joined with other matter in the universe. Every tetrahedral energy wave state within us depends on the in-waves and out-waves of every other wave state. Our brains and other parts of our neural physiology are interconnected by this unseen communication network, which coordinates and regulates behavior of certain parts of the body. This interconnection is all pervasive and instantaneous. The manifestation of this energy comes from the 'empty' vacuum, known as the quantum vacuum.

'Potential' only manifests when we provide the frequency information through our thoughts and intentions of what we want to create. It is unlimited potential and therefore what we are capable of creating is also unlimited.

The energetic link that we all share explains how our intentions, thoughts, and prayers can travel to a sick friend and connect with their mind and consciousness. It also explains why every action is followed by a reaction. Everything that happens to one energy wave-state affects every other wave-state. Therefore, all of our actions and thoughts have ramifications throughout the unified fabric of spacetime.

'Ourselves' is a collection of cells in the same way as a collection of 'ourselves' makes up a society. Therefore, our relationship with others, in fact, is having a relationship with ourselves. We are the same. We arise from the same vibration that manifests as spacetime consciousness. This is why the people in our lives are always pushing our buttons. They are a mirror to us and to who 'we' think we are. When we don't like what we see it is because we don't like what we see within our own self.

The Möbius Coil

Scalar waves can be created by wrapping electrical wires around a figure eight in the shape of a möbius coil. When an electric current flows through the wires in opposite directions, the opposing electromagnetic fields from the two wires cancel each other and create a scalar field (figure 31).

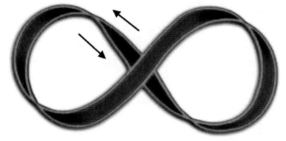

Fig. 31. A möbius coil produces scalar waves.

Valerie hunt explained that the human body produces bio-scalar waves. I was determined to find where in the body opposing currents of energy exist. I started my search by looking for biological möbius coils. That is how I found cellular supercoils. The DNA antenna in our cells' energy production centers (mitochondria) assumes the shape of what is called a supercoil.[139] Supercoil mtDNA look like a series of möbius coils (figure 32). Recent evidence suggests that disruption of the supercoiled structure is associated with functional changes in animal mitochondria and act as a marker for oxidative damage.[140] The möbius coil configuration suggests that supercoil mtDNA may generate scalar waves.

---

139 Kamenetskii F, *Unraveling DNA*, (Perseus Books, 1997)

140 Jinsong C, Kadlubar F F, Chen Z C, (2007) *DNA supercoiling suppresses real-time PCR: a new approach to the quantification of mitochondrial DNA damage and repair.* (http://www.ncbi.nlm.nih.gov/pmc/articles/PMC1851651/) Retrieved 29 Nov 2011

Scalar Heart Connection™

Fig. 32. Supercoiled DNA molecule.

There is another möbius coil configuration found within the vascular system. The continuous flow of blood through the arterial system—which runs next to the venous system but in opposite directions—contains möbius coil properties. The circulation of blood throughout the body also resembles the figure-eight shape of the möbius coil. Within the vascular möbius coil there are subsets of the figure eight along the major capillary networks. These major capillary networks are associated with primary organs and are related to the endocrine glands (figure 33).

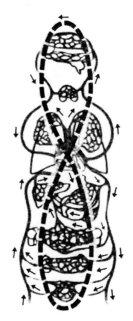

Fig. 33. The circulatory möbius coil has figure-eight intersections across each of the chakras.

The Möbius Coil

The diagram above illustrates how the chakra centers correspond to the figure-eight intersections of the vascular bio-möbius coil system. At the heart of this system is the heart. The heart muscle sets up the strongest electromagnetic field of the body. Consequently, there is ample energy flowing through the vascular figure-eight system to set up a bio-scalar field. Perhaps the largest bio-scalar generator is the heart itself. There is an intersection of venous blood passing through the right atrium, overlapping aortic blood coming through the left atrium. The möbius coil intersection occurs just in front of the lungs, which contain a huge web-like network of capillary connections (figure 34). It is tempting to believe this capillary network acts as a battery for the storage of scalar waves. Hence, the reason most ancient healing traditions stress the importance of breathing.

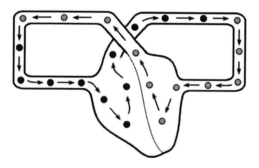

Fig. 34. The flow of blood moving through the heart and lungs in a figure-eight.

Scalar waves generated in the body may protect us from the negative effects of solar radiation and other harmful electromagnetic stresses from the environment by constantly canceling out these harmful non-bio-energetically compatible frequencies. Scalar waves generated in the body might also provide an energetic communication system that connects all cells. Some of the benefits of scalar waves are confirmed by scientists. In one study, scalar waves created a twenty-fold stimulation of cell growth in human immune system cells.[141]

It was going to be some time before I found the möbius coil in the spine. Fortunately, my search led me to the möbius coil of the heart and I now saw how the heart connects to all the chakra centers and their associated organ systems. The same scalar waves generated by the scalar field of the heart connect to the field of unlimited potential arising from the chakra centers. Our connection to this field explains why Valerie Hunt insisted we have the ability to direct energy from the quantum field to activate enzymes that target proteins to carry out specific tasks. It shed light on the mechanism of the heart's connection to Universe and unlimited intelligence/potential.

Candace Pert, in her book, *Molecules of Emotion*, explains that the opiate receptors on cell membranes function as sensing molecules, dancing and vibrating to the vibrations of other molecules of emotions.[142] When the signaling molecule is in resonance with the receptor molecule, it acts like a key that opens the cell membrane lock where the vibratory message is delivered deep into the interior of the cell. This sets off a chain of biochemical reactions based on the nature of the message.[143] Recall her description of the chakras as sites dense with neuropeptide transmitters. These are signaling molecules that transmit information to vibrating cell surface receptors, which have specific effects on behavior. The area of the heart contains every known neuropeptide.[144] The heart

141 Rein G, *The Body Quantum: Non-classical Behavior of Biological Systems*, "The Resonance in Residence Science Addendum," Ilonka Harezi, 2002.
142 Pert C, *Molecules of Emotion; The Science Behind Mind-Body Medicine*, (Touchstone, 1999), p. 23
143 Ibid., p.24
144 Pert C., *Your Body is Your Subconscious Mind*, Study Guide, (Sounds True, 2000), p. 7

sends these vibrating molecules of emotion out through its figure-eight möbius coil circulation system as it connects with all the cells in our body. When we breathe, the brain also releases all the known peptides into the bloodstream.[145] This is why Dr. Clarissa Pinkola Estés, in her book, *Women Who Run With the Wolves*, says taking a breath is to feel our emotions and, likewise, when we don't want to feel, we stop breathing and hold our breath instead.[146] Recall how the heart and breath synchronize in a perfect musical minor third ratio. Together, the heart and lungs create a figure-eight möbius coil (figure 34) that can harmonize the entire body-mind system.

Pert says our body-mind uses cues from neuropeptides to retrieve or repress emotions and behaviors. In this way, memory is encoded at the level of the receptors and is emotion-driven and unconscious.[147] It is from these unconscious memory patterns held within the body-mind that we make decisions that shape our experience in every conscious moment. When our decisions are influenced by unconscious memories of our traumatic history we often make choices that are not always in our best interest. Pert contends that when our emotions are blocked due to repressed memories, blood flow to the brain can become chronically constricted.[148] As a result, we may become stuck and unable to respond to our environment except by repeating old patterns conditioned by past negative experiences.[149] Cellular memory of traumatic events can disrupt coherent energy flow and communication throughout the body-mind, including organs as well as the brain. Dr. Ryke Geerd Hamer found by means of x-rays,

---

145 Pert C, *Molecules of Emotion; The Science Behind Mind-Body Medicine*, (Touchstone, 1999), p. 186-187
146 Estés C P, *Women Who Run With Wolves; Myths and Stories of the Wild Woman Archetype*, (Ballantine Books, 1992), p. 336
147 Pert C, *Molecules of Emotion; The Science Behind Mind-Body Medicine*, (Touchstone, 1999), p. 143
148 Ibid., p.289
149 Ibid.

EEG, CT Scans, and pathology that every tumor patient he reviewed had a cystic structure in the brain.

Hamer theorized that these cysts are located in specific areas of the brain associated with emotions and feelings. He believes unresolved emotions can lead to energetic blocks in the brain and associated organs, and these blocks may be behind the development of tumors in those organ areas.[150]

William Redpath, in his book, *Trauma Energetics: a Study of Held-Energy Systems*, says subtle energetic representations of trauma are resolvable if the person is able to allow themselves to go deep into the trauma and sort out the unresolved event. The person must renegotiate the meaning of the dark places, "where the negative energy is stored."[151] To accomplish this, we need a way to enter the body-mind's internal conversation so we can tune in to the vibrations of our emotions. Sufi poet, Rumi wrote that deep listening allows us to hear greetings from the secret ones inside the heart. The branches of your intelligence, he says, grow new leaves in the wind of this listening. As the brightness of the Infinite's light loves to illuminate space and time, so does its song love to sing to the deep ear in your heart.[152] We can consciously attune to the coherent rhythms that are innate within us and couple with the energy field of the Earth and Universe.

Pert describes meditation as a way of consciously entering the body's internal conversation and interacting with its biochemical processes.[153] Meditation can relax our active and stressful brain waves into phase with theta frequencies. Recall that theta brain waves are in the 5 to 8 Hz range. We

150 Hamer R G, *Summary of the New Medicine*, (Amici di Dirk, 2000)

151 Redpath W, *Trauma Energetics: a Study of Held-Energy Systems*, (Barberry Press, 1995)

152 Jalā al-Dīn Rūmī, Maulana, *The Glance: Rumi's Songs of Soul-Meeting*, Trans. Coleman Barks, Penguin Compass, 1999, p. 90

153 Pert C, *Molecules of Emotion; The Science Behind Mind-Body Medicine*, (Touchstone, 1999), p. 263

The Möbius Coil

learned earlier that the heart chakra frequency of 528 Hz, when divided by 72 heartbeats per minute, is 7.3 Hz; an ideal heart-brain entrained frequency. This is also in the range of the frequency of the Earth-ionosphere resonance cavity of 7.8 Hz. Just in case we are still not convinced of the power of the Solfeggio frequency of 528, consider that 528 is the 48th harmonic of 11 (the Sun flare cycle). And, 528 is the 27th harmonic of Mercury's circumference frequency rate of 19.557 Hz.[154] The relationship of 528 to a celestial body other than the Moon or the Sun suggests there are more coincidences yet to be discovered. For example, John Martineau points out that the orbits of Mercury and Venus contain the geometry of the Tetrahedron (figure 35).

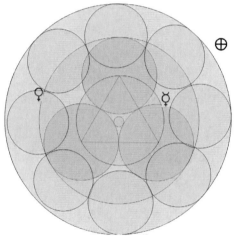

Fig. 35. Mercury's mean orbit passes through the center of three circles outlined by the mean orbit of Venus.[155]

When we meditate, we have the opportunity to enter the domain of the planets and the scalar field of Universe.

---

154 Light travels 19.557 times around the median circumference of Mercury per second.
155 Martineau J, *A Little Book of Coincidence*, (Walker & Company, 2002), p. 20

Universe is anxious to reveal itself. John Martineau is helping us see the signs. In another example, he shares that the mean orbits of Mars and Jupiter create four touching circles and a square, similar to the concept of 'squaring the circle' (figure 36).

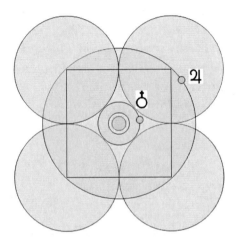

Fig. 36. Mars and Jupiter's mean orbits.[156]

When we enter the domain of the planets and the celestial geometries, through either meditation or entrainment with theta brain waves, we often arrive to the arena of the subconscious. This is where we find our deepest psychological material suppressed and hidden away. According to Sophy Burnham, *The Art of Intuition*, theta frequencies take us into deep meditation and mystical experiences and have healing potential.[157] She also says that alpha waves (8 to 12 Hz) act as a bridge between the conscious and subconscious mind.[158] This bridge occurs at around 8 Hz, which is the frequency be-

156 Martineau J, *A Little Book of Coincidence*, (Walker & Company, 2002), p. 41
157 Burnham S, *The Art of Intuition: Cultivating Your Inner Wisdom*, (Tarcher/Penguin, 2011), p. 149
158 Ibid.

tween theta and alpha. The number 8 is the number of notes that makes an octave, hence the term 'octave' ('eight' from the Latin: octo).[159] The 66th harmonic above 8 Hz happens to be exactly 528 Hz. The number 6 reminds me of the hexagram and the Twin-Tetrahedrons. When we attune our inner vibrations to 8 Hz we come into phase with the natural rhythms of Universe. This helps explain why people whose brain waves often border between theta and beta (around 8 Hz) usually have low anxiety and low neuroticism.[160] These people seem to have found a balance between emotional and active, logical thinking (problem solving).[161]

But what if we are not able to achieve such a balance due to worry, upset, or other negative emotions? How can we access our inner dialogue if we are not able to quiet our outer dialogue? We attempt to reach that calm theta state but our overactive mind is stuck in emotional reactions and old behavior patterns. Often, we experience pain or unease, but are not conscious of the source. It is not so simple to enter our inner landscape and find hidden psychological material. That is why we call it 'subconscious.' But what if Metatron's Cube is more than a symbol? Perhaps, Metatron's Cube is also the key to unlocking the subconscious material that is preventing us from moving forward in life-enhancing ways. What if there is something more remarkable about the number 8?

---

159 c.1300, *vtaues* (pl., from popular O.Fr. form *otaves*), later reformed, from M.L. *octava*, from L. *octava* dies "eighth day," fem. of *octavus* "eighth," from *octo*. Originally "period of eight days after a festival," also "eighth day after a festival" (counting both days, thus if the festival was on a Sunday, the octaves would be the following Sunday). Verse sense of "stanza of eight lines" is from 1580s; musical sense of "note eight diatonic degrees above (or below) a given note" is first recorded 1650s, from L. *octava (pars)* "eighth part." (http://www.etymonline.com/index.php?term=octave) Online Etymology Dictionary. Retrieved Dec 6, 2011
160 Aubele T, Wenck S, Reynolds S, *Train Your Brain to Get Happy: The Simple Program That Primes Your Grey Cells for Joy, Optimism, and Serenity*, (Adams Media, 2011), p. 38
161 Ibid.

Vector Equilibrium

"Humanity is equally incapable of seeing the nothingness
from which they emerge
and the infinity in which they are engulfed."[162]
~ Blaise Pascal

Metatron's Cube is a symbol of wholeness. The Solfeggio frequencies and their triangulations cause the geometries of Metatron's Cube to actualize in spacetime. Metatron's Cube also represents that everything in Universe moves and vibrates around our heart. It also represents the geometry of the heart itself. Furthermore, it contains the resonance of the emotional qualities inherent in the chakras. As such, it may be more than a symbol. It may serve as a tool for personal transformation; a template for uniting the individual to the global community, with Earth and Universe. It may in fact be the geometry and ground of spacetime. We are not aware of this geometry because it is invisible to us. It is invisible because we cannot see equilibrium. To find the geometry of equilibrium in the twin-tetrahedrals inherent in Metatron's Cube we will need help from Fuller.

Fuller coined the term Vector Equilibrium. Typical of

---

162 The actual quote is: "... what is man in the midst of nature? A nothing in comparison with the infinite, an all in comparison with nothingness: a mean between nothing and all. Infinitely far from comprehending the extremes, the end of things and their principle are for him inevitably concealed in an impenetrable secret; equally incapable of seeing the nothingness whence he is derived, and the infinity in which he is swallowed up." *The Thoughts, Letters and Opuscules of Blaise Pascal*, O.W. Wright (trans.), (Hurd and Houghton, 1869), p. 160.

Scalar Heart Connection™

Fuller's complex language, he describes it as an omnidirectional closest packing of equiradius spheres around a nuclear sphere (figure 37).[163] That makes 12 equal spheres placed symmetrically around one sphere. That equals 13 closest packed spheres (the number of spheres in Metatron's Cube; the number of full Moons per year):[164]

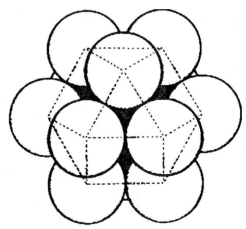

Fig. 37. Omnidirectional closest packing of spheres defining nodes of the Cuboctahedron.

Take the spheres away and we are left with the geometry of the Cuboctahedron, which consists of 8 Tetrahedrons converging toward a common center in perfect symmetry equilibrium. Fuller called it Vector Equilibrium or VE because it is the only geometric form where all the energy lines (vec-

---

163 Fuller R B, *Synergetics: Explorations in the Geometry of Thinking*, (Macmillan Publishing Company, 1978), p. 116

164 At Jesus Christ's last supper, there were thirteen people around the table, counting Christ and the twelve apostles.

In Judaism, 13 signifies the age at which a boy matures and becomes a Bar Mitzvah.

In the Mayan Tzolk'in calendar, trecenas mark cycles of 13 day periods.

There are 13 cards in a suit.

The number of colonies that formed the United States.

Vector Equilibrium

tors) are of equal length and strength. They represent the energy of attraction and repulsion. The illustration below (figure 38) does not show the Tetrahedron in the front or the one in the back. I drew it this way to highlight the geometry of singularity:

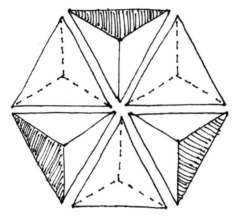

Fig. 38. Vector Equilibrium.

The actual geometry below (figure 39) reveals 12 converging lines (the zodiac) where all forces balance out evenly, creating stillness.

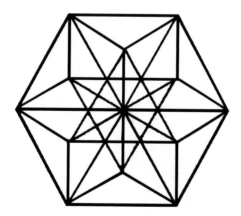

Fig. 39. Cuboctahedron

Scalar Heart Connection™

The geometry of the Vector Equilibrium, complete with its contractive force, lies directly in the center of the Star-Tetrahedron (figure 40). First, we must re-orient ourselves back to the Octahedron that we first saw in figure 5:

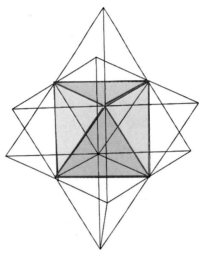

Fig. 40. The common cavity created by the interlaced Tetrahedrons creates the Octahedron.

Within the Octahedron is nested the Vector Equilibrium of the Cuboctahedron (figure 41).

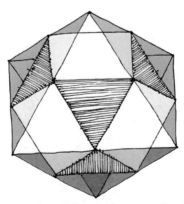

Fig. 41. The Vector Equilibrium is nested within the common area (Octahedron) of the Star-Tetrahedron.

Vector Equilibrium

It is easier to see this if we view it within the context of the Star-Tetrahedron (figure 42).

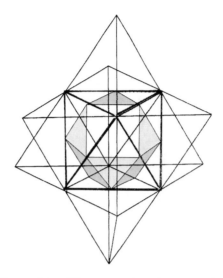

Fig. 42. The Vector Equilibrium nested inside the Octahedron within the Star-Tetrahedron.

Physicist Nassim Haramein also studied Fuller. In his DVD, *Crossing the Event Horizon,* Nassim illustrates how the Vector Equilibrium is inherent in the Twin-Tetrahedrons of Metatron's Cube. He built up his Star-Tetrahedron one Tetrahedron at a time. He used 20 single Tetrahedrons to make one large Tetrahedron. The two interlaced Tetrahedrons, therefore, consist of 40 small Tetrahedrons. We are already getting the idea of the fractal nature of this geometry. Haramein found equilibrium by adding 3 more Tetrahedrons to each of the 8 stars found at the points of the Star-Tetrahedron. He now had 64 Tetrahedrons (the original 40, plus 3 x 8 = 24. 40 + 24 = 64). What emerges from this geometry are Tetrahedrons radiating outwardly into the infinitely large and Tetrahedrons contracting inwardly into the infinitely small. Haramein referred to it

Scalar Heart Connection™

as the fundamental structure of the vacuum state geometry.[165] The image below (figure 43) shows how the inward forces of the Cuboctahedron balance with the outward forces of the outward pointing Tetrahedrons that make up the Star-Tetrahedron.

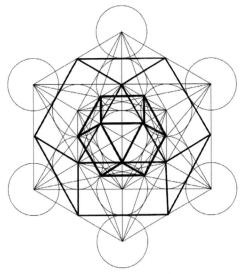

Fig. 43. The geometric structure of the quantum vacuum.

Within the Star-Tetrahedron, radiation and implosion symmetrically unite inside the same manifold, generating the dual torus topology of spacetime. We now have zero-point and infinite potential within a framework that repeats itself in harmonic intervals or octaves. Note that the radius of the inner Cuboctahedron is the radius of the outer (8 tetrahedral geometries in an octave proportionate to one another, ad infinitum). This geometry is self-repetitive and defines the scale of objects we see in space, from subatomic waveforms to galaxies.

The radiation and implosion within the Star-Tetrahedron is represented by Yin and Yang, and the swirling vortices

---

165 *Crossing the Event Horizon*, www.theresonanceproject.org

of the chakras. Most torus dynamics contain two tori acting like male and female aspects – one spiraling toward the North Pole and its opposite spinning toward the South Pole. This is the Coriolis Effect, which we see in the Earth's weather patterns and the plasma flow of the sun. We saw earlier, from Jenny's work, how vibration causes a complexity of motion and wave dynamics that manifest the Star-Tetrahedron (figure 44).

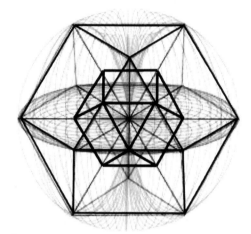

Fig. 44. The torus flow of energy dynamics between the inner and outer Vector Equilibrium geometry.

We don't observe the VE in the physical world because it is the geometry of absolute balance. What we experience on Earth are the force dynamics radiating toward or contracting away from equilibrium. The VE is the imaginable, yet invisible, archetype of all shapes and symmetries we see in the world, including the heart.

By placing hundreds of electrodes around the human heart, Arthur Winfree, of the University of Arizona, discovered that the heart's electrical field takes the shape of a torus.[166]

166 Winfree A T, *When Time Breaks Down: The Three Dimensional Dynamics of Electrochemical Waves and Cardiac Arrhythmias*, (Princeton Press, 1986)

Scalar Heart Connection™

Heart cells are unique in that they produce strong electromagnetic signals extending as far as twelve to fifteen feet from the body in the shape of a torus (figure 45). Winfree illustrates the geometrical origins of the electrochemical waves of the heartbeat as specifically a 7-color torus-donut.[167] The Earth, Solar System, Galaxy, and perhaps even Universe form the shape of a torus. "Some scientists conjecture that all energy systems from the atomic to the universal level are toroid in form. This leads to the possibility that there is only one universal torus encompassing an infinite number of interacting, holographic tori within its spectrum."[168]

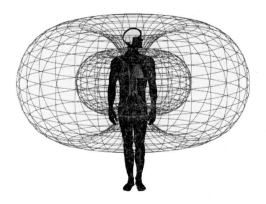

Fig. 45. The torus flow of the heart's electromagnetic radiation. (Courtesy: Institute of HeartMath)

It has been suggested that the torus can be used to define the workings of consciousness itself. The torus allows a vortex of energy to form which bends back along itself and re-enters itself. Therefore, the energy of a torus is continually refreshing itself, continually influencing itself, and conscious of itself.

---

167 Ibid.
168 Pearce J C, *The Biology of Transcendence: A Blueprint of the Human Spirit*, (Park Street Press, 2004), p. 58

Vector Equilibrium

I believe the force that gives rise to torque and spin, and the geometry of the fabric of spacetime, is the Cosmic Vibration or Music of the Spheres. Physicist Amit Goswami says the Cosmic Vibration is consciousness and that consciousness is the ground of all being.[169] Goswami describes quantum physics as the physics of possibilities, which is an outgrowth of the whole wave-particle duality problem. This is the standard way of looking at quantum physics; that everything we choose to look at causes the waveform of possibilities to convert into actualities. This is fun to consider because it can mean that by changing how we see things we can materialize all our hopes and dreams. However, Goswami makes a valid argument that the eyes we see with, through our brain, are already actualities. Well, he doesn't say it exactly like that. In the 2009 film documentary, *Quantum Activist*, he describes it more like: "Consciousness is not made of brain; brain is made of consciousness." In other words, our brain, which is already material, is not causing consciousness to convert into material objects. It is consciousness that has already chosen this possibility. Goswami argues that we can only choose how to observe and how to react.[170]

Goswami further elucidates that our individual ego consciousness makes choices based on past learning and what we have already experienced. He says the conversion of possibility into actuality happens at the subtle level of our consciousness.[171] The subtle level of our consciousness is nonlocal consciousness. Our real consciousness is behind the ego at the level of Cosmic Consciousness. This consciousness is who we really are. Goswami says, "This nonlocal consciousness, in the process of creating, becomes the object that we ob-

---

169 Goswami A, *How Quantum Activism Can Save Civilization*, (Hampton Roads Publishing Company, 2011), p. 53
170 *The Quantum Activist*, Film Documentary, 2009
171 Ibid.

serve and also the subject."[172] Said differently, we are Cosmic Consciousness falsely experiencing ourselves as non-Cosmic Consciousness.

A fourteenth century poem by Mahmud Shabistari, called the *Gulshan-i rāz* or *Garden of Mystery*, provides an illustration that our physical world is the reflection of the light of this Cosmic Consciousness. The example asks us to imagine how a burlap cloth placed over a lamp would cause specks of light to shimmer on a nearby wall. Each individual speck of light would see itself as a separate self-determined and independent being. Because of their limited view, they would believe they are on their own and left to ensure their own survivability. The specks of light on the wall might be full of anxiety, worry, even fear and act out in strange and unbecoming ways: steeling from other specks of light, calling each other names, or forming into groups; dividing themselves into countries by drawing artificial borders on the wall and then starting wars with specks on the other side of their border. They would tend to cling to the constituents of matter, believing that is all there is and that the pursuit of desires and pleasure is the purpose of their existence. What the specks would not see, with their limited perspective, is the unifying light emanating from the lamp. If they could see with their inner vision that they are in fact one with the light they would no longer cling to the plaster on the wall. They would also see themselves in all the other specks.

> You and I are 'accidents' of the Essence of Being,
> like openings in the covering of the lamp of Being.

> Know all light as the same, whether of spirits or bodies,
> sometimes shining from the mirror, sometimes the lamp.[173]

---

172 Ibid.
173 Shabistari M, *Garden of Mystery* (*The Gulshan-i rāz of Mahmud Shabistari*), Trans. Robert Abdul Hayy Darr, (Archetype, 2007), p. 66

Vector Equilibrium

The good news is that if we can alter our state of con-sciousness so that it resonates with Cosmic Consciousness, then our intentions can come true. At that level, there is no ego in between and our intentions become the same as the intentions of Cosmic Consciousness. Achieving this level of consciousness requires that we move out of the domain of the lower chakras. We can help ourselves by consciously trying to entrain with the frequencies of the heart, which are harmoni-ous with theta waves in the brain, the resonance of the Earth, cycles of the Moon, Sun, and Universe.

We saw earlier how our heart torus is hierarchically nested in the tetrahedral matrix of spacetime. This suggests that our heart is connected to, and affects, every other to-rus system in Universe, from galactic tori to subatomic tori. Since the heart sits at the center of this torus hierarchy, one could argue that Cosmic Consciousness flows first through the heart. As Goswami points out, our consciousness comes first. Therefore, it is consciousness that manifests the heart. When we entrain the heart to the frequency of consciousness, we become consciousness. When we are influenced by nega-tive emotions, we lose coherence with Cosmic Consciousness. When we are out of phase with Cosmic Consciousness, our heart torus impinges on the natural harmony of Earth and Universe. Consequently, when we look at what has happened to the environment, we are seeing a reflection of our inner state. When we are out of tune within ourselves and with each other, the external environment mirrors that back to us in the form of war, terrorism, economic collapse, starvation, poverty, natural disasters, etc., etc.

If emotional imbalances create abnormal vibratory patterns in our heart torus, then it must be possible to ask our heart how to regain balance and equilibrium. Reconnecting to the inherent harmony of our heart is the objective of Scalar Heart Connection™.

Scalar Heart Connection™

Metatron's Cube provides a template for accessing the innate wisdom of the heart. The field of neurocardiology has confirmed that the heart is a sensory organ that is a center of information processing that allows it to learn, remember, and make functional decisions independent of the cerebral cortex.[174] Researchers at the Institute of HeartMath have found that while experiencing negative emotions such as anger or anxiety, heart rate variability becomes more erratic and disordered. On the other hand, positive emotions, such as love, appreciation, or compassion produce coherent patterns in the heart's rhythms.[175] [176] Increased heart-brain synchrony results in increased system-wide energy efficiency and conservation of metabolic energy supporting the link between positive emotions and improved health.[177] Essentially, the heart will always tell us what we need to know. We only need to know how to ask and how to listen.

Scalar Heart Connection™ utilizes the geometry of Metatron's Cube to access the heart's innate knowing. The

---

174 Armour J, Ardell J. *Neurocardiology*. New York: Oxford University Press, 1994

175 McCraty R, *The Energetic Heart: Bioelectromagnetic Interactions Within and Between People*, (Institute of HeartMath, 2003), p. 3

176 An optimal level of heart-rate variability (HRV) is key to cardiovascular function, flexibility, and adaptability. Reduced HRV can be pathological. Heart-rhythm coherence refers to an orderly and harmonious organization of rhythms in information processing. See *The Coherent Heart; Heart-Brain Interactions, Psychophysiological Coherence, and the Emergence of System-Wide Oder*, by Rollin McCraty, Ph.D., Mike Atkinson, Dana Tomasino, and Raymond Trevor Bradley, Ph.D. (Institute of HeartMath, 2006).

177 Salovey P, Rothman A, Detweiler J, Steward W. *Emotional states and physical health*. Am Psychol 2000; 55; 110-121

system helps identify those subconscious beliefs and attitudes that hold us in limitation, preventing us from experiencing joy and inner connection.

Scalar Heart Connection™ is easy to use and fun to experience. It helps people identify disharmonies within the chakras and meridian energy channels. A lack of coherence within these energy systems weakens the resonance pattern of what we want to manifest in our lives. Once we move out of resonance with stress, depression, and self-sabotaging vibrations, we can strengthen the energy patterns and thought-forms that are life enhancing.

Scalar Heart Connection™ incorporates the geometry of Metatron's Cube. The goal of the process is to arrive at an inner equilibrium similar to how the interlaced Tetrahedrons, when balanced, create the Octahedron (figure 46).

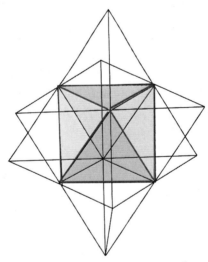

Fig. 46. The Octahedron emerges from the common area shared by the interlaced Tetrahedrons.

Recall how the color spectrum comes together to form a harmonious white light. By lining up the Solfeggio Codes to their respective chakras and assigning them to the faces of the

Scalar Heart Connection™

Tetrahedrons, we have a blue-print that can guide us to inner equilibrium (figure 47).

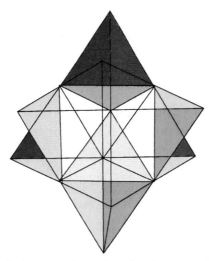

Fig. 47. The chakras assigned to the faces of the Twin-Tetra-hedrons represent balanced emotional equilibrium.

When the heart's Twin-Tetrahedron geometry is co-herent and harmonious, the resulting equilibrium allows our heartbeat to match the beat of other hearts, the earthbeat, and the orchestra of Universe. This geometry illustrates the heart's connection to the chakras, which can over-activate (emotions) from certain mind-brain perceptions and memories. Memory activated emotions arising from past trauma or other upsets reinforce correlated limbic and neocortical brain circuits.[178] These emotional feelings flow through the chakras and rever-berate through the corresponding organs. Heightened energy flowing through the chakras is what we experience as feel-ings.[179] It is only later that the mind tries to give meaning to

178 Goswami A, *How Quantum Activism Can Save Civilization*, (Hampton Roads Publishing Company, 2011), p. 82
179 Ibid., p. 80

these feelings. When the mind cannot integrate or fully digest the meaning, it replays the event repeatedly until mind-brain circuits become rutted and static. These are the circuits we then filter our present day experiences through causing us to become stuck in negative emotions of anger, resentment, fear, and anxiety – to name a few. These feelings keep us focused on the lower chakras, which are normally involved with instincts and survival. This tends to move our attention (self-consciousness) out of the higher chakras, whose feelings are associated with unconditional love, charity, clarity, and contentment. In order to re-pattern negative mind-brain circuitry, we need to first identify where the feeling energy is over-activated. Only then can we hope to convert negative emotions into positive ones. The model below (figure 48) provides the framework for identifying the area of upset or imbalance.

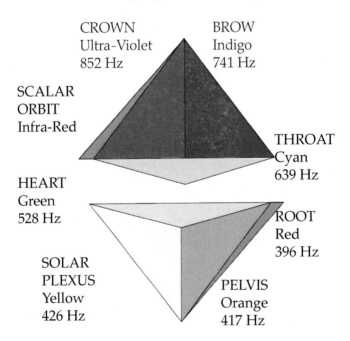

CROWN
Ultra-Violet
852 Hz

BROW
Indigo
741 Hz

SCALAR
ORBIT
Infra-Red

THROAT
Cyan
639 Hz

HEART
Green
528 Hz

ROOT
Red
396 Hz

SOLAR
PLEXUS
Yellow
426 Hz

PELVIS
Orange
417 Hz

Fig. 48. Twin-Tetrahedrons, the Chakra Aspects, and Solfeggio frequencies (Quantum Healing Codes™)

Scalar Heart Connection™

The heart is connected to the field of nonlocal consciousness. Therefore, the heart is aware of the subconscious material patterned in our brain circuitry from old beliefs arising from earlier experiences, traumas, and societal conditioning. These patterns often cause us to habitually react to our environment in negative or non-productive ways. Our negative behavior patterns resonate with negative outcomes. Though we are sometimes aware that our actions are self-fulfilling, we feel doomed as we helplessly attempt to break the brain-circuit patterns that lead to these unfruitful outcomes. Fortunately, the heart is aware of these negative memory patterns. For this reason, we have the possibility of re-routing these circuits by overlaying them with positive emotional frequencies and establishing/shifting these old patterns.

Metatron's Cube provides a template for methodically uncovering the negative frequencies. It also provides the frequencies needed to change these patterns into positive ones. By mapping out the emotional aspects associated with each chakra and their organ relationships, we have a means for identifying both the subconscious content holding us in negative patterns as well as the positive aspects required to shift our perspective. When we change our perspective, we change our reality.

When we feel emotionally out of balance, we can use Metatron's Cube as a means to connect to the heart's innate knowing. The process allows us to do a 'session' on ourselves as well as for and with someone else. After identifying the emotional discomfort arising from negative beliefs and outcomes, the 'heart-mediator' asks the 'recipient' to pick a number from a list in order to identify the specific chakra that is over-activated. For some, it is not different from picking a playing card out of a deck of cards. Others experience an intuitive sense of what number is involved. I have found that numbers come to me as mental pictures, like playing cards. At other times, I visualize a row of numbers and wait to see if one stands out amongst the others. This is an individual process. The heart is imaginative and creative. How it communicates and tells us which number to pick is ever changing.

Picking numbers related to our inner psychic/emotional state is somewhat similar to The *I-Ching*. Jung described the system of The *I-Ching* as a method devised by which an inner state can be represented by an outer one; in this case a written statement about our subconscious emotional state, which is assigned to a number.[180] Like The *I-Ching*, the only criterion of validity of the method is the observer's opinion that the text of the statements chosen reflects a true rendering of their psychic/emotional condition.[181] Number, as we have seen throughout this book, and as Jung explained, is the predestined instrument for creating and apprehending an already existing orderedness.[182]

The Scalar Heart Connection™ method asks the 'recipient' to pick a number related to the chakra that is out of balance in relation to the objective of the session. The 'heart-mediator' reads aloud what the corresponding number represents as well as the name of the chakra. This allows the recipient's brain (frontal cortex) to process the insight given by the heart. The heart knows and is patiently waiting for the brain to make the connections necessary to heal the wound and associated negative belief patterns. Next, the 'heart-mediator' asks them to pick a number, usually one to five, related to the emotional quality of the chakra that has been identified. This is where the process begins to earn trust and acquire validity. It often happens that the 'recipient' picks a number and discovers that the emotional quality is the same as the feeling

---

180 Jung C G, *Synchronicity: An Acausal Connecting Principle*, from Vol. 8. of the Collected Works of C. G. Jung, (Princeton University Press, 2010), par. 865, p. 36

181 Jung C G, forward to *The I-Ching* Trans. Wilhelm R, Bollingen Series XIX (Princeton University Press, 1997), p. xxv

182 Jung C G, *Synchronicity: An Acausal Connecting Principle*, from Vol. 8. of the Collected Works of C. G. Jung, (Princeton University Press, 2010), p. 40

Scalar Heart Connection™

they had earlier expressed as their motivation for wanting the session in the first place. For example, one 'recipient' wanted a session around feelings of fearing the unknown. The number she picked as the imbalanced chakra was the number representing the root chakra. The related emotion she picked next was 'fear.' Another 'recipient' wanted a session around feelings of betrayal and mistrust. Her heart also directed her to the root chakra. However, in this case, the emotional quality she chose was 'low self-esteem.'

At this point, the 'recipient' is consciously aware of the chakra that is out of balance and more specifically, the underlying emotion causing the energetic disruption. The next step is to obtain more information about the aspect of the chakra that is expressing negative emotions. This is the negative conditioned belief or perspective that has habitually patterned itself in the mind-brain. We also need to identify the positive emotion or belief, which will be used to replace the negative pattern belief. By now, the 'recipient' is beginning to see the underlying issue. In the first example above, after the 'recipient' addressed her fear of the unknown, they chose the number related to the negative statement: "I exploit nature and her natural resources." The positive statement she chose was: "I welcome and embrace change." I share this because I know the reader is searching for continuity between these two statements. It is this need for a rational explanation that shakes the core of the compulsive mind-brain circuits. Now, the 'recipient' is not only seeing the underlying issue, but they are also beginning to understand and accept it. This is a powerful process because it allows communication between the heart and the brain, which allows the 'recipient' to not only see the connections but to feel and understand the connections as well.

There are organs associated with most of the chakras. The organs reflect various and specific aspects of the chakra emotions. In the case of the root chakra, the associated organ, or meridian system, is the large intestines. In the example of the first 'recipient,' they chose the large intestines statement: "I know when to move on." A story is now emerging from the depths of her unconscious.

In order to re-wire the negative circuits, it is generally necessary to identify the origin of the negative belief. This is the exciting part, because both 'heart-mediator' and 'recipient' know they are embarking on a journey that will lead them to deeply buried subconscious material. The process is designed to lead the 'recipient' to specific areas of their past. The heart may lead them to a specific month when they were in the womb or to the birth process itself. Others may need to identify an ancestral or genetic belief, a specific age, person involved, and/or an event. Others still, may be lead to a past life trauma or to a negative situation their mind-brain has repressed.

I found that the heart always knows just how deep to go. The heart never takes ego-consciousness deeper than it is capable or willing to go. It is an automatic safety stop. The heart safely guides us to the 'aha' moment where consciousness becomes aware of what has been unconscious up to this point. Once the origin of the negative pattern emerges, we can consciously change our perspective by reflecting on the past event or circumstances with the lens of compassion and understanding. In the earlier example with the 'recipient' whom we established feared the unknown, they chose to look at the sixth month of being in the womb. When asked why they thought their heart brought this to their attention, she said, "Because my mother was young, nervous, and afraid of caring for me." She now became conscious of how she entrained with the resonance of fear coming from her mother. Her mind-brain circuits responded with the memory of using nature to seclude herself. This is exploitation, but in a subtle sense. She was also unable to move forward or to embrace change because of the resonance of 'the fear of the unknown.'

The 'recipient' now has a picture of how their emo-

Scalar Heart Connection™

tional responses and behaviors have been conditioned by past events. The Scalar Heart Connection™ process provides space for the 'recipient' to reflect on what their heart has illuminated to conscious awareness. Our sample 'recipient' has figured out that she becomes paralyzed when she gets caught up in her head, trying to figure out the pieces before taking action. She does this, not in a healthy and precautionary way, but because she is afraid of the unknown. She realizes that she compulsively tries to make sure whatever she does is done right and is completely thought out ahead of time in order to be safe. She is afraid to be wrong, so she remains frozen as life goes on around her.

At this point in the process, the 'recipient' is asked to create a positive statement that reflects how they will move forward in a fresh, life-enhancing, and positive manner. This aspect is crucial as the 'recipient' now must reach deep into their mind-brain circuits and envision how 'things' will be different – positive – going forward. The very fact that they come up with a positive statement at all is a huge achievement. It means they now have a conscious choice in responding to similar circumstances in the future. They can choose to respond in the same old way or they can now choose to respond positively based on their new insights. In many cases, this new insight is enough to shift old patterns into new and positive patterns. The 'recipient' in our example created her positive statement that read: "I fearlessly go out into the world, where I am exposed to life's ever changing joys and unknown adventures."

Just in case more information is required, the process provides an opportunity to ask the heart if we need something more. Often, the heart will want to reinforce the new positive intention by having the subject listen to a Quantum Healing Code™. When this comes up, we ask the heart to choose which one they need. Generally, the code that the person chooses from the list is the code related to the chakra found to be out of balance, but not always. It can also be the case that they need another code or frequency. Recall how the frequencies and their harmonics came together in ways that produced the triangles found in the geometry of Metatron's Cube. We might view emotional imbalance as creating distortions in the geometry of ego-consciousness, which manifest as disruptions in heart patterns. This distortion, which is really only a question of perspective, causes us to lose coherence with nonlocal consciousness. Therefore, when we listen to a specific Quantum Healing Code™ within the context of our newly created positive statement, we are reformatting the geometry of inner-connection.

This brings us back to the image of the mandala. The mandala reminds us that our experiences help bring us from the outer edges of ego-consciousness back to the center of the mandala, to the center of wholeness, unity and equilibrium. Equilibrium is the white light center of the Twin-Tetrahedron, where the double-heart becomes one heart. At this stage, we automatically resonate with the intentions of non-local Cosmic Consciousness.

Putting it All Together

We learned in the first chapter (Vibration Creates Geometry) that recent scientific studies show that the heart receives more information than the brain. The heart contains a mini-brain with an independent complex system of neurons and neurotransmitters that receive and respond to the flow of chemicals from our thoughts and emotions. The heart also communicates with the brain and other cells in the body energetically through electromagnetic field interactions. The signals (chemical, hormonal, frequency modulation, etc.) the heart sends to the brain influences perception, emotional processing, as well as cognitive functioning. The heart responds to information it receives in the brain and checks it for accuracy, literally functioning like a small voice that ensures our actions are from a place of wisdom. It also nudges us when it senses danger or feels we are coming from a place of non-integrity.

When we ignore the wisdom of our heart and allow brain-consciousness to dominate, we may find toxic emotions and thoughts suppressed deep within our cells.[183] This can cause the entire body to feel burdened and out of rhythm with the harmony of love, peace, and well-being.

The oscillations of a love-filled heart are harmonious with the calm, creative and insightful theta-waves of the brain (see chapter eight: Scalar Waves). Our heart rate is also in resonance with the earthbeat of Earth, and the harmonies of our solar system and beyond (see chapter six: Quantum Healing Codes™).

The heart-center of harmony, innate wisdom, uncon-

---

183 Leaf C, *Who Switched Off My Brain*, (Thomas Nelson, 2009)

ditional love, and well-being is the Fourth Chakra, which sits in the center of the body's seven chakras (see chapter seven: The Double Heart). The color of the heart chakra is green. The color green lies at the center of the visible light spectrum in the range of 528 THz (terahertz). Each of the chakras relate to one of the seven colors of the rainbow:

Chakra	Color	Color Frequency in THz
Root	Red	396
Pelvis	Orange	417
Solar Plexus	Yellow	426
Heart	Green	528
Throat	Cyan	639
Brow	Blue	741
Crown	Violet	852

The Chakras and their Color Correlations.

An Ancient symbol for the heart chakra is the Star-Tetrahedron, which is also the geometry of Metatron's Cube (see chapter four: The Geometry of Number):

Putting it All Together

Indian yoga heart chakra symbol.

In chapter six (Quantum Healing Codes™) we discovered that the frequencies of the chakras found in the Quantum Healing Codes™ fit the triangles within the geometry of the heart chakra:

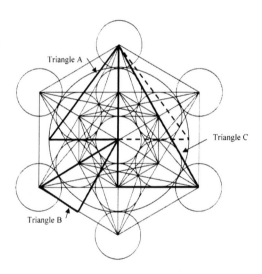

Triangle A is frequency 396 and its octaves;
Triangle B is frequency 396, 417, 639;
Triangle C is frequency 417, 639, 741

Scalar Heart Connection™

Is it possible the Ancients knew that the heart contains all the information from the other chakra emotional centers? The heart chakra symbol they used contains the frequencies associated with the chakra colors. These frequencies, when treated as lengths of triangles, fit together to form the Star-Tetrahedron symbol (Metatron's Cube).

When we view the heart chakra as a harmonious geometry containing the color aspects of all the chakras combined, we can better imagine what the heart might look like when one of the chakras is out of balance due to a repressed or unresolved (unassimilated) emotional conflict/trauma.

When we scale the color frequencies from terahertz to cycles per second, we arrive at audible frequencies. This conversion gives us the same heart chakra Star-Tetrahedron but in a musical form. Now we can imagine the discord in the heart from one or another imbalanced chakra as an orchestra out of tune. The frequencies scaled down to the audible range are available as the Quantum Healing Codes™ in a CD format (see resources at the end of this book). The codes contain the frequencies 396, 417, 528, 639, 741, and 852.

The Scalar Heart Connection™ system utilizes the Star-Tetrahedron/Metatron's Cube geometry and the heart's innate wisdom to identify the color or musical note (from the Quantum Healing Codes™) that is out of balance or out of tune. Our emotions and suppressed negative thoughts often find ways to get our attention through pain and discomfort – physical or otherwise. These unresolved emotional conflicts can also influence our behavior and hence our relationships, both personal and professional. The examples below of actual Scalar Heart Connection™ sessions will help illustrate how we can ask the heart to identify subconscious and negative emotions and behavior patterns. The process will also utilize the heart's innate knowing to identify what we need in order to shift these negative resonances into positive and life-enhancing vibrations.

Putting it All Together

Mary

Mary owns her own business and wants to increase her income in a way that will give her more time to pursue her creative interests. She is unable to imagine, or resonate with the thought that she can grow her business without increasing her personal involvement. Consequently, she feels stuck, discouraged, and disheartened.

The Scalar Heart Connection™ system (SHC) directs her to pick a number one through seven. She closes her eyes and feels a number come from her heart and into her awareness. The number is seven, which is the root chakra. This tells us that the root chakra is the source of the discomfort and negative mind-conditioning belief around this issue of time-freedom. The color of the root chakra is red, which is the frequency of 396 cps according to the Quantum Healing Codes™. This means that the Star-Tetrahedron geometry of the heart is in a state of disharmony because the color red is diminished or the musical vibration is out of tune.

As we explore deeper into the source of the discord, the SHC system instructs Mary to pick a number related to an emotion associated with the root chakra. She picks the number related to 'Low Self-Esteem.' The SHC system then instructs her heart to pick a number related to the negative brain-conditioning that allowed the issue to remain unresolved. The number Mary picked relates to the statement: "I am unsafe in the world." The positive message her heart wanted her to become aware of, and to integrate the resonance of, was: "I face life with courage and trust."

The chakras also connect to various organs. The root chakra connects to the Large Intestines. The SHC system, therefore, asked Mary to pick a number related to the emotions and energies of the Large Intestines. The number she picked related to the statement: "I am flexible and avoid being overly critical, exacting or compulsive."

Next, the system wants to make Mary aware of how she holds this issue in her body. She picks the number related to 'psychological.' The statement associated with this level for Mary is 'depression.'

The SHC system now wants to identify how this negative belief/response first entered Mary's mind-body system. To obtain this information the system asks Mary to pick a number related to an 'Earlier Experience.' The number she picked relates to the birth process, specifically to the eighth month in the womb. As a result of the negative influence she picked up in the womb, a more positive resonance was not integrated. This is called the 'Unmet Heart Need.' Mary picked a number for the 'Unmet Heart Need' related to: "Peace."

Often, certain outside things, places, people, etc. can trigger the negative belief and create a whole cascade of unresolved emotions. In Mary's case, the number her heart picked for 'Triggers' was related to "Places."

At this point in the session, we have gained enough information and insight from the heart that Mary is able to put together a story of what she believes her heart is trying to tell her. Mary recalls that when she was young her mother was often worried about having enough to survive. Mary felt certain this might be the belief she entrained with when she was in her mother's womb at eight months. Moreover, her mother acted out her worry with compulsively cleaning the house, whether it needed it or not. She felt that cleaning was a way of contributing to her survival. Consequently, Mary was taught to clean house every Sunday as a matter of course. In a moment of realization Mary said, "My compulsiveness around being involved in my business is driven by my need to be needed and recognized. Being needed is how I know I am working and surviving."

The SHC system then asked Mary to put together a positive statement, something she needed to resonate with in order to shift the old pattern into one that is life enhancing and in alignment with her goals. She reflected for a moment and said, "I face life with courage and trust."

In order to anchor the new positive resonance around courage and trust, Mary picked a number in the SHC system related to making new brain-circuit connections. The modality that Mary picked was track number eight of the Quantum Healing Codes™, which is frequency 396 and 528 combined into a chord. Frequency 396 relates to the root chakra and the color red, while 528 is the color green related to the heart chakra. Mary listened to the tone for three minutes with her eyes closed, contemplating and feeling the new resonance now entering her life.

Afterwards, she said she no longer felt worried about her survival and not having enough money. She felt she could finally let go of the need to control her business and allow new ways of increasing her creativity time into her life.

Anne

Anne was concerned about the pain in her knees as well as her general health. The aspect of the heart's Star-Tetrahedron that was out of balance was the pelvis chakra. The number Anne's heart picked for the over-activated emotion was the one for 'Lust.' The imbalanced mind-brain conditioning statement was: "I am never satisfied." And the positive resonance needed to bring this to balance and harmony was: "I value and appreciate myself just as I am." The organ statement needed came from the kidneys: "I express my emotions appropriately." Anne was holding the resonance of this emotional conflict on an energetic level. The SHC process identified it as a "sympathetic response causing her to suffer."

The Earlier Experience was during the birth process. Similar to Mary's session above, Anne's issue also arose in the eighth month in the womb. The Unmet Heart Need was

"Creativity." The trigger that generally activated this latent emotional conflict was "Situations."

Anne used the information she gained from the SHC session to put a story together about how her Earlier Experience set in motion the negative belief she was holding in her body-mind system. She recalled that her mother lived on a farm when she was pregnant with her. She also knew that her mother was not happy about living on the farm, nor did she enjoy the community and its various social gatherings and networks. Her mother loved the city and its excitement, etc. This reminded Mary of the last tea party she attended in her small rural town. She said she went into a tirade over wearing a dress for the party. She was aware at the time that her outburst was unreasonable and felt pity for her husband, who gave her complements on how she looked in an effort to calm her down. Her belief at that time was: "I look ugly in dresses." Anne then related that she had issues of anorexia previously. She said, "I have an image of myself and am always comparing myself to others."

Anne now realized that she wanted to shift the resonance around this negative belief about herself. The positive statement she created for herself was: "I am content with myself just as I am and I move forward boldly with my creative ideas."

The SHC session helped Anne identify that the reason she was not able to actualize this positive statement in her life was her subconscious fear that she had to be better than she was in order to be loved ("I am always comparing").

To anchor the positive resonance in her body-mind system, Anne needed to breathe-in the positive and breathe-out the old negative belief. Recall from the chapter on Scalar Waves how the heart and breath synchronize in a perfect musical minor third ratio. When we breathe, the brain also releases all the known peptides into the bloodstream. Together, the heart and lungs create a figure-eight möbius coil that can harmonize the entire body-mind system.

At the end of her session, Anne related how she has had kidney/bladder problems her entire life. She now understood how it was related to the emotional imbalance she was holding onto in her pelvis chakra. She also made a connection with why "Lust" came up at the beginning of her session. She admitted that she loves cake and has a lustful relationship with cake. Fortunately, she was now resonating with being content – with herself.

Pamela

Pamela was having health issues, which she believed her son was causing. Her thirty-something year-old son had recently moved in with her after losing his job. The son was demanding and often seemed unreasonable in his expectations of what his mother could provide for him. Pamela said she tried to set boundaries, but her son waits until she is vulnerable to challenge her. "It is all my fault. I can't fix it," she said.

I asked her to pick a number, one through seven. She chose four, the number related to the heart chakra. The heart chakra emotion she chose was 'possessive.' The negative aspect resonating in the heart chakra was: "I am only interested in myself, not the interest or well-being of others." And the positive aspect needed was: "I feel my connection with the planet and its inhabitants." This seemed a bit harsh, especially for someone struggling to improve her relationship with her grown child. We had to continue and trust the heart's wisdom. I asked her to choose a number related to the organ-meridian associated with the heart. Her heart chose the heart meridian. It is clear now that this is most definitely an issue of the heart, which most mothers would have already guessed. I asked her to choose the heart-meridian statement needed for this session. She chose the statement: "New ideas flow through my heart."

I asked Pamela to choose the number associated with the earlier experience involved. She chose 'genetic / ancestral.' I then asked her if she had a 'feeling' as to why her heart picked 'genetic / ancestral.' Without hesitation, she told me the whole story.

Pamela said she 'felt' as though she might have been a warrior in a past life. In this case, 'genetic / ancestral' referred to her own ancestral past, as in 'past life' memory. She thought, perhaps, that she and her son were both medieval warriors with swords and armor and the whole works. She paused and reflected that her past was probably the reason she was in law-enforcement in the present. She said, "I don't want to wear my armor anymore."

I then asked her to pick a number related to the 'unmet heart need' that arose from her past life experience. I call this the Heart Bill of Rights. We are all entitled to certain rights related to what our heart expects and deserves. In this situation, she chose the number related to 'forgiveness.' Her heart did not experience forgiveness. She was not resonating with the frequency of forgiveness because she did not have that experience in the past.

Pamela now needed to come up with the 'story.' She needed to sort out the clues her heart had provided and come up with what she needs in order to shift the old mind-brain circuits. She said she was tired of fighting. She recalled that even when she was young the neighborhood kids tried to hang her. She later married a man who tried to kill her and their three-year-old son. She said the two of them fled the husband and lived in their car. The statement that came up earlier: "I am only interested in myself, not the interest or wellbeing of others," now explains itself. She had to be only interested in herself in order to survive these events. She also became aware that her love for making stained glass as a hobby has to do with working with the anvil. "I love to pound metal on the anvil," she said. It makes her feel like a blacksmith pounding on swords.

She then needed to create a positive statement from the information and insights she had received from her heart. She came up with the statement: "I am open, warm, non-threatening; I am safe, creative and loving." She then commented that she could now see that her son still wants to fight, "It's like he loves the sound of swords clanging together. He antagonizes me, tries to provoke me into a fight because that is the only way he knows how to relate to me." She said she needed to surrender, just wave a white flag. Then she commented on how odd it was that she was holding a white dishcloth at the moment. "Yes, I need to wave this at him."

When I asked her to pick a number related to a modality to help embed the positive statement she created for herself. She chose number ten. Ten relates to 'none.' This indicated that she had already shifted her perspective. I asked her to pick a number related to a positive action that might be needed. She picked the number ten again, which in this case corresponds to 'other.' It felt right to suggest that when she feels frustrated with her son to go into her workshop and bang on her anvil. I stressed banging in slow, rhythmical beats related to a calm heart. This was her call 'to retreat.' As long as she holds the space of surrender in the relationship, mother and son will have to find more positive ways to relate to each other.

I followed up with her three months later. She wrote:

The session was so timely as my son and I were struggling so much. Identifying the source of the struggle and aggressiveness from past lives and the simple remedy of waving the white flag in surrender to diffuse it was perfect. Then the rhythmic pounding on the anvil is so calming and soothing for me. It was not an immediate change, but doing it at every confrontation diffused it so well. Our relationship has moved into another calm level and we are finally taking the time to know who each of us actually is, not what we think we see. Thank you!

~ Pamela

Tommy (age 6)

Tommy experienced a large earthquake when he was four-years-old. After the earthquake, even the slightest aftershock or loud noise caused him to become hysterical.

When asked to choose a number related to the chakra still over-activated by this experience, he picked the number related to the heart. The negative mind-brain circuit pattern was, "I am unable to receive the love given by others." The positive mind-brain message needed to shift this was, "I give and receive unconditional love."

This feeling was manifesting on the psychological level and the sub-category he chose was, 'Obsessive Compulsive.'

The number he picked for the earlier experience that gave rise to this mind-brain circuit was 'in the womb.' The unmet heart need, or the positive resonance that did not reach the developing heart, was 'Devotion.'

The word 'devotion' is sometimes hard for children to comprehend. Tommy related better to 'love and protection,' particularly in the context of how his parents were devoted to loving and protecting him. When asked who else loves him and protects him, he responded, "God." In this sense, Tommy needed to make the connection that he could trust that he was taken care of.

The word 'devotion' brought in a power greater than Tommy's parents, whom he knew were not as powerful as earthquakes. The idea of devotion also adds a component of nonindividual self. Perhaps, on a subconscious level, Tommy needed to re-connect with a power that is both himself and outside himself. He needed to plug in, so to speak, to receiving and giving unconditional love.

The SHC system then guided him to breathe in the feeling of being protected by God. This helped reinforce the new resonance of 'receiving unconditional love."

The following day, an aftershock rumbled through the house. Tommy's mother observed that Tommy continued to play, unaware of the shaking that before sent him compulsively into an uncontrollable fit.

Tommy's situation is a good example of how a change in perception, arising from conditioned mind-brain circuits, changes our response. The situation was the same (an aftershock), but Tommy's conditioned response was now re-wired out of old belief responses into new and positive perceptions of the same stimulus. Becoming aware of the unmet heart need of 'devotion' caused Tommy to shift his fear and feel protected. As a result, he was aware of the aftershocks, but no longer reacted hysterically.

Rose

Rose was concerned that she was suppressing anger, not because she felt angry, but because her heart told her in an earlier SHC session that her feelings of depression related to repressed anger. That session raised her awareness to the possibility that she was not being honest with herself about her emotions. She started her new session by picking the number related to the brow chakra and the number related to 'restlessness.' The statement she chose related to the imbalanced or non-coherent belief resonating in her mind-brain circuits was: "I constantly brood over problems." This struck a deep chord with her as she often found herself compulsively worrying about her future.

The positive statement she chose was: "My inner voice communicates with me clearly and willingly." She also needed a specific brain resonance. The one she chose was: "Miracles are a natural part of my life." The session revealed she was suppressing anger on the level of spirit. The spirit related statement was: "I am disconnected from God / Universal Consciousness."

The deeper question was how this disconnect arose in her subconscious in the first place. Was there a situation in her past that her cells responded to emotionally but were not able to integrate because the mind-brain was unable or unwilling to extract the higher essence of the situation?

Rose chose the number corresponding to a genetic or ancestral experience. In other words, she was born into this pattern. The genetic pattern was subconsciously determining her behavior. Next, she chose the Unmet Heart Need, which for her was: "Freedom from confinement." When asked if she could identify with the story her heart was communicating, she began by recounting that her grandmother's parents had divorced. She suspected that her grandmother never got over the feeling that her father left her. Her grandmother and her great-grandmother survived because her older brother worked to support them. Her grandmother soon married a man who provided for her; a man she had to please, otherwise she would be left on her own without a means of support. In time, her grandmother's resentment consumed her.

Rose suddenly saw the pattern. She said, "If I express my anger, I won't be loved. If I'm not loved, no one will take care of me." She realized that brooding over her problems is a mental trap. "I do it because otherwise I won't be safe from people who are mad at me. They won't love me anymore and I'll be stuck in a bad situation."

Recalling that the Unmet Heart Need was "freedom

from confinement," Rose said, "I want to be free to love and be loved, but when my parents divorced, my mom told me there was no such thing as unconditional love. I remember how I tried extra hard to please my mom, and especially my dad whenever I could visit him."

The 'story' allowed Rose to create a positive and life-enhancing statement: "I am connected to my higher self, which guides me fearlessly and freely through my life's experiences."

Rose connected to a new pattern; one that permits her to follow her dreams without feeling her survival depends on pleasing others or suppressing what is true for her.

Rose became aware how the old genetic pattern had affected other family dynamics including her mom's behavior, her sister's, and potentially her nieces' as well. She was also relieved that by changing the genetic pattern for herself, she was also changing it for her future children and the generations to follow.

Monica

Monica was having difficulty losing weight. She explained that when she looked in the mirror she didn't recognize herself and it seemed that no matter what she did she couldn't seem to lose weight. She felt like an emotional component was involved, so she asked for a Scalar Heart Connection™ session. She began her session by taking in a deep breath and centered into her heart saying, "I trust my heart's innate intelligence."

Letting her heart guide her, Monica chose the number representing the heart chakra. The emotion related to the heart chakra was needy. This resonated with Monica, so she continued to find the imbalanced mind-brain conditioning causing her problem. Her heart guided her to the statement:

"I disappoint others." The positive aspect needed to balance this was: "I love myself and others unconditionally." The organ meridian out of balance was the lung. The positive statement needed for the lungs was: "I breathe in life fully."

Next, her heart guided her to the emotional level and the specific emotion was terror. The session revealed that the earlier experience was a collective consciousness or society belief. Monica immediately knew that this collective consciousness was related to her family.

Her heart's unmet need was creativity. Before creating her story and positive statement she identified her cellular memory trigger as behavior. This was just one more piece to the puzzle and now she was eager to express her story.

In one way, she was desiring acknowledgment for her success and her talents, but she felt that if she let people, more specifically her family, know that she was successful, she would have to provide for them and they would start to expect too much from her. She realized she believed that if her family knew just how successful she was, she wouldn't fit in with them and perhaps they wouldn't love her for herself but would only depend on her for security. She also reflected on her difficulty breathing, sharing that sometimes it is as though she forgets to breathe at all.

Now that her heart has shared with her mind-brain consciousness that she is constantly trying to be less than she is for the sake of others, she was able to create the positive statement: "I love myself and others unconditionally and breathe in life fully." Both statements resonated with Monica, but it was still possible that there was a secondary gain involved, preventing the embedding of her new positive belief. The secondary gain confirmed what she came up with in her story: "If I change, I'll abandon those I love." While she wanted to breathe in life fully and share her success with her family, she felt that she would no longer fit in and even abandon them. By pretending to be less successful, she realized she began to

Putting it All Together

entrain with that belief, to the point of affecting her outward appearance.

Without shifting the subconscious belief around holding on to extra weight, it was unlikely that any amount of dieting would work in the long run. In order to embed the new positive belief, Monica needed to listen to the Quantum Healing Codes™. Finally, she needed to reinforce her new positive belief with a positive action: breathing.

Conclusion

Life's challenges provide opportunities for transformation. They often force us to seek refuge and guidance with our nonindividual self. Yet, it is the Heart of Understanding, the Buddha self, that we find difficult to access in our conditioned responses to personal affronts.

Scalar Heart Connection™ is only one of many tools that we can utilize to help us reconnect with our inner creativity, where our moment-to-moment responses align with intuitive and unitive consciousness.

For some, this may become the first step on the ultimate transformative journey of complete surrender and unification with non-being consciousness. For the rest of us, reconnecting with the inner voice of inter-connected consciousness feels like a must if humanity is going to survive the 21st Century. With unitive consciousness, our future actions and behaviors will only be appropriate and life-enhancing actions – for the planet and the global community.

Appendix

On the Geometry of the Periodic Table

Robert J. Moon (1911-1989) was a physicist and nuclear scientist. He played a key role in the Manhattan Project and was a founding member of the Fusion Energy Foundation. According to his hypothesis on the atomic nuclear structure, protons are the vertices of the nested structures of the Platonic solids. The 'Moon Model' is consistent with much of the same experimental date that underlies the periodic table of the elements. However, mainstream science does not embrace his geometric presentation of the periodic table, as it seems to be inconsistent with the evidence from spectroscopy, upon which the accepted conception rests.[184] However, new quantum numbering diagrams using a fractal structure based on the Tetrahedron, Dual Tetra, Octahedron and Cube exactly matches the same order shown by the sequence from experimental spectral data.[185] Meaning, there are other ways to view the periodic table beyond the mass number.

Maria Göeppert-Mayer shared the Noble Prize in Physics for proposing the 'shell model' of the structure of the atomic nucleus. In her Nobel lecture, she said the model was born from a thorough stud y of the experimental data, which demonstrated a remarkable pattern. "The pattern emerges," she said, "if one plots properties against either the number of

---

184 Hecht L, *Advances in Developing the Moon Nuclear Model*, 21st Century, Fall 2000

185 Borg X, *The Particle – The wrong turn that led physics to a dead end*, Blaze Labs Research, (http://blazelabs.com/f-p-develop.asp). Retrieved 09 Nov 2011

neutrons, or the number of protons in the nuclei, rather than against the mass number."[186] She described the numbers as "magic numbers." The numbers are 2, 8, 20, 28, 50, 82, 126. She discovered the numbers by a sudden intuitive revelation.[187]

Xavier Borg, inspired by Linus Pauling's attempt to reverse engineer the magic number sequence into a geometric progression, solved the problem by assuming the nucleus contains the closest and most stable stacking structure – the Tetrahedron (figure 6).[188]

Fig. 6. Close-packed Tetrahedron

By considering that nuclei build up as double tetrahedral structures, Borg was able to compute the "magic number" series by counting the number of stacked Tetrahedrons in each layer and multiplying by a factor of two. At the fourth layer, he had to account for the overlapping layer of the interlaced dual Tetrahedrons. By subtracting the shared Tetrahe-

186 Göeppert-Mayer M, *The Shell Model*, Nobel Lecture, December 12, 1963
187 von Franz M, *Number and Time*, (Northwestern University Press, 1998), p. 47
188 Borg X, *The Particle – The wrong turn that led physics to a dead end*, Blaze Labs Research, (http://blazelabs.com/f-p-magic.asp). Retrieved 09 Nov 2011

Appendix

drons occurring at the fourth layer, he was able to agree with
Göeppert-Mayer's shell model (figure 7).

Level (n)	2	2	3	4	5	6	7	8
Tetrahedron number (level n)	1	4	10	20	35	56	84	120
Less triangular shared layer (level [n-1])	-	-	-	6	10	15	21	28
Total nucleons per tetrahedron	1	4	10	14	25	41	63	92
Total nucleons per double structure Z (magic number)	2	8	20	28	50	82	126	184

References

1 Jung C G, *Memories, Dreams, Reflections,* (Vintage Books, 1989), p. 302

2 Ibid.

3 Campbell J with Moyers B, *The Power of Myth,* (Anchor Books, 1991), p. 234

4 Goswami A, *The Self-Aware Universe; How Consciousness Creates the Material World,* (G. P. Putnam's Sons, 1993)

5 Einstein A, Leopold I, *The Evolution of Physics,* (Touchstone, 1967), p. 31

6 Bohm D, Basil, Hiley J, *The Undivided Universe: An Ontological Interpretation of Quantum Theory,* (Routledge; reprint edition, 1995), p. 35

7 Venkatesananda S, *The Concise Yoga Vasistha,* (State University of New York Press, 1985), p. 68

8 Venkatesananda S, *The Concise Yoga Vasistha,* (State University of New York Press, 1985), p. 68

9 Buckminster Fuller R, *Synergetics: Explorations in the Geometry of Thinking,* (Macmillan Publishing Company, 1978), p. 103

10 Ibid., p. 81

11 Ibid., p. 71

12 Ibid., p. 83

13 Ibid.

14 Ibid.

15 Ibid., p. 84, 85

16 Weber R, ed., *Dialogues With Scientists & Sages: the Search for Unity,* (Routledge and Kegan Paul, 1986), p. 18

17 Shabistari M, Trans. Robert Abdul Hayy Darr, *Garden of Mystery (Gulshan-I rāz),* (Archetype, 2007), p. 204

18 Einstein A, *Sidelights on Relativity,* An address delivered on

References

May 5, 1920, in the University of Leyden, Kessinger Publishing, p. 10-11

19 Wolff M, *Exploring the Physics of the Unknown Universe*, (Technotran Press, 1990), p. 178

20 de Broglie D, *The Wave Nature of the Electron*, Nobel Lecture, December 12, 1929

21 Einstein A, *Ideas and Opinions*, (Broadway, 1995), p. 285

22 Wolff M, *Exploring the Physics of the Unknown Universe*, (Technotran Press, 1990), p. 114

23 Ibid., p. 114

24 Ibid., p. 180

25 Ibid.

26 Lawlor R, *Homage to Pythagoras: Rediscovering Sacred Science*, (Lindisfarne Books, 1994), p. 46

27 Jenny H, *Cymatics Volume 2*, (Basilius Presse, 1974), p. 183

28 Ibid.

29 Volk J, *From Vibration to Manifestation: Assuming our Rightful Place in Creation*, The Quester; Autumn 2010, p. 4

30 Jenny H, *Cymatics Volume 2*, (Basilius Presse, 1974), p. 97

31 Ibid., p. 169

32 Bohm D, edited by Lee Nichol, *The Essential David Bohm*, (Routledge, 2007), p. 3

33 Plato, *Timaeus*, par. 38a

34 Ibid., par. 54c-d

35 Jenny H, *Cymatics Volume 2*, (Basilius Presse, 1974), p. 161

36 Ibid., p. 165-166

37 Plato, *Timaeus*, par. 57e

38 Ibid., par. 58a

39 Ibid., par. 57e

40 Einstein A, *Einstein on Cosmic Religion and Other Opinions & Aphorisms*, (Dover Publications, 2009), p. 33

41 Heraclitus, *The Complete Fragments*, Trans. and Comments by William Harris, Middlebury College, frag. 64

42 Jenny H, *Cymatics Volume 2*, (Basilius Presse, 1974), p. 183

43 Kaku M, *The Universe is a Symphony of Vibrating Stings*, You-

Tube, posted by bigthink, 31 May 2011

44 Ibid.

45 Plato, *Timaeus*, par. 54a

46 Buckminster Fuller R, *Synergetics: Explorations in the Geometry of Thinking*, (Macmillan Publishing Company, 1978), p. 4

47 Jung C G, *Aion; Researches Into the Phenomenology of the Self*, Bollingen Series, CW 9 Vol. II, (Routledge & Kegan Paul, 1959). See Chapter: "The Structure and Dynamics of the Self."

48 *Matthew* 6:21

49 Marie-Louise von Franz, *Number and Time*, (Northwestern University Press, 1998), p. 45

50 Jung C G, *Synchronicity: An Acausal Connecting Principle*, Collective Works Volume 8, (Bollingen Foundation, second edition, 1969) par. 870, p. 456

51 Ibid.

52 McCraty R, *The Resonant Heart, Shift: At the Frontiers of Consciousness*, Dec. 2004 / Feb 2005, p.15

53 Plato, *Timaeus*, par. 37a – 38b

54 Jean-Pierre Mahé, "Preliminary Remarks on the Demotic "Book of Thoth" and the Greek Hermetica" Vigiliae Christianae 50.4 (1996:353-363) p.358f. "There are many parallels with Egyptian prophecies, with hymns to the gods or other mythological texts, and with direct allusions, the closest comparisons can be found in Egyptian wisdom literature, characteristically couched in words of advice from a "father" to a "son".

55 Hermetica, *Asclepius III*, (Solos Press ed.), p. 136

56 Leet L, *The Secret Doctrine of the Kabbalah*, (Inner Traditions, 1999), p. 8

57 Hall M, *The Secret Teachings of All Ages: An Encyclopedic Outline of Masonic*, Hermetic, Qabbalistic and Rosicrucian Symbolical Philosophy, (CreateSpace, 2011), p. 42

58 Eder A, *The Star of David: an ancient symbol of integration*, (R. Mass, 1987), p. 22

59 Ibid., p. 23

References

60 Ibid., p.22

61 Jung C G, *Psychology and Religion*, Bollingen Series XX (Princeton University Press, 1969), par. 150

62 Jung C G, *Memories, Dreams, Reflections*, (Vintage Books, 1989), p. 196

63 "Metatron." Encyclopædia Britannica. Encyclopædia Britannica Online, Retrieved 11 Nov. 2011

64 "Enoch walked with God; then he was no more, because God took him away." [*Genesis* 5:24]

65 ". . .the person of Enoch, who after a lifetime of piety, was raised, according to legend, to the rank of first of the angels or literally: prince of the divine face, or divine presence. "God took me . . . to the heights of the seventh heaven." [Extract of 3 Enoch.] Gershom G. Scholem, Major Trends in Jewish Mysticism (Schocken, 1995) p. 67.

66 Scholem G, *Major Trends in Jewish Mysticism* (Schocken, 1995) p. 67. [Extract of 3 Enoch.]

67 *Genesis* 17:1-19

68 *Exodus* 23:21

69 Epstein P, *Kabbalah: The Way of the Jewish Mystic*, (Barnes & Noble, 1998), p. 93-94

70 Leonora Leet, *The Secret Doctrine of the Kabbalah*, (Inner Traditions, 1999), p. 113

71 Jung C G, *Psychology and Alchemy*, Bollingen Series XX, (Princeton University Press, 1977), par. 165

72 Schneider M, *A Beginner's Guide to Constructing the Universe*, (Harper Perennial, 1995), p. 214

73 Schneider M, *A Beginner's Guide to Constructing the Universe*, (Harper Perennial, 1995), p. 214-215

74 Martineau J, *A Little Book of Coincidence*, (Walker & Company, 2002), p. 30

75 NASA, science.nasa.gov, (http://science.nasa.gov/science-news/science-at-nasa/2002/18jan_solarback) Retrieved 17 Nov. 2011

76 Plato, *Laws V*, 737 e

77 For more information on the Greek unit of measure related to the circumference of the Earth, see *The Acropolis Width and Ancient Geodesy*, by Nicholas Kollerstrom, The International Journal of Metrology, Fall 2005, p. 38-41 (www.dioi.org/kn/stade.pdf) Retrieved 22 Nov 2011

78 The Pythagorean skein is basically a way of transforming written language into a mathematical code. This allowed Pythagoras to convey ancient secrets in an encrypted manner that would keep the power of his mysterious knowledge out of the hands of people who would use it for destructive and coercive purposes.

79 NASA, science.nasa.gov. (http://science.nasa.gov/science-news/science-at-nasa/2000/ast03apr_1m/) Retrieved 17 Nov 2011

80 Hancock G. and Bauval R., *The Message of the Sphinx*, (Three River Press, 1997), p. 37

81 Chang J J, Fisch J, Popp FA, *Biophotons*, (Kluwer Academic Publishers; Dordrecht, 1998)

82 Mae-Wan Ho, Fritz Albert Popp, Ulrich Warnke (editors), *Bioelectrodynamics and Biocommunication*, (World Scientific Publishing Co., 1994), p. 270

83 Ibid., p.272 (276-277)

84 F. A. Popp et al., Recent Advances in Biophoton Research and its Applications, eds. F. A. Popp et al., (World Scientific, Singapore, 1992)

85 Ibid.

86 Lipton B, *The Biology of Belief Course Book*, 2003, p.48

87 Wordsworth, C F, *Identifying Less-Coherent Patterns*, (Wordsworth Productions, March 2000 edition)

88 Lipton B, *The Biology of Belief Course Book*, 2003, p.48

89 "Solfeggio" - The French or Italian system in which the sol-fa syllables are used to correspond to the notes of the scale of C major.

90 Goldman J, *Healing Sounds-The Power of Harmonics*, (Element, 1994)

References

91 Electroencephalography (EEG) is the recording of electrical activity along the scalp. EEG measures voltage fluctuations resulting from ionic current flows within the neurons of the brain.

92 Burnham S, *The Art of Intuition: Cultivating Your Inner Wisdom*, (Tarcher/Penguin, 2011), p. 149-150

93 Ibid.

94 McCraty R, *The Resonant Heart, Shift: At the Frontiers of Consciousness*, Dec. 2004 / Feb 2005, p.16

95 Ibid., p. 151

96 Tesla N, (1905) "The Transmission of Electrical Energy Without Wires As A Means Of Furthering World Peace" *Electrical World and Engineer,* January 7: 21–24

97 Oschmann J, *Energy Medicine - The Scientific Basis*, (Churchill Livingstone, 2001), p. 185

98 O'Keefe J, Nadel L, *The Hippocampus as a Cognitive Map*, (Clarendon Press; Oxford 1974)

99 Jung C G, *Psychology and Alchemy*, Bollingen Series XX (Princeton University Press, 1977), p. 128

100 Dolnick B, *Enlighten Up: The Keys to Kabbalah*, (New American Library, 2005), p. 75-76

101 Leet L, *The Secret Doctrine of the Kabbalah*, (Inner Traditions, 1999), p. 172

102 Campbell J, *The Inner Reaches of Outer Space*, (Perennial Library, 1988), p. 87

103 There are 432,000 years in the present cycle of time, the so-called Kali Yuga. See Joseph Campbell, *The Inner Reaches of Outer Space*, (Perennial Library, 1988), p. 35

104 Information provided by John Stuart Reid, CymaScope. com

105 Campbell J, *The Inner Reaches of Outer Space*, (Perennial Library, 1988), p. 87

106 Leet L, *The Secret Doctrine of the Kabbalah*, (Inner Traditions, 1999), p. 91

107 Venkatesananda S, *The Concise Yoga Vasistha*, (State Univer-

sity of New York Press, 1985), p. 142

108 Leet L, *The Secret Doctrine of the Kabbalah*, (Inner Traditions, 1999), p. 174

109 Ibid.

110 Anodea J, *Eastern Body, Western Mind : Psychology and the Chakra System as a Path to the Self*, (Celestial Arts, 1996), p.5

111 Gerber R, *Vibrational Medicine*, (Bear & Company, 1988), p.128

112 Matsumoto K, Birch S, *Extraordinary Vessels*, (Paradigm Publications, 1986), p.6

113 Pert C, *Molecules of Emotion; The Science Behind Mind-Body Medicine*, (Touchstone, 1999), p. 21-22

114 Pert C, *Your Body is Your Subconscious Mind*, (Sounds True, 2000)

115 Ibid.

116 Ibid.

117 Ibid.

118 Hunt V, et al., A Study of Structural Integration from Neuromuscular, Energy Field, and Emotional Approaches, Rolf Institute of Structural Integration, 1977.

119 Eden D, *Energy Medicine*, (Jeremy P. Tarcher/Putnam, 1998), p.146

120 Ibid p.149

121 *Dr. Berkowsky's Six Element Paradigm Workbook*, (Joseph Ben Hil-Meyer Research, Inc., 2010), p.22

122 Eden D, *Energy Medicine*, (Jeremy P. Tarcher/Putnam, 1998), p.148

123 Ibid., p. 152

124 Ibid.

125 Ibid., p. 153

126 Ibid.

127 *Dr. Berkowsky's Six Element Paradigm Workbook*, (Joseph Ben Hil-Meyer Research, Inc., 2010), p.23

128 Jung C, edited by Jaffe A, *Memories, Dreams, Reflections*, (Vintage Books, 1989), p.248

References

129 Eden D, *Energy Medicine,* (Jeremy P. Tarcher/Putnam, 1998), p.156

130 Ibid., p. 157

131 Ibid., p. 159

132 Ibid., p. 160

133 *Dr. Berkowsky's Six Element Paradigm Workbook,* (Joseph Ben Hil-Meyer Research, Inc., 2010), p.26

134 Ibid.

135 Oschman J, *Energy Medicine; the Scientific Basis,* (Churchill Livingston, 2001), p. 204

136 Ibid., p. 203

137 Ibid., p. 206

138 Ibid., p. 207

139 Kamenetskii F, *Unraveling DNA,* (Perseus Books, 1997)

140 Jinsong C, Kadlubar F F, Chen Z C, (2007) DNA supercoiling suppresses real-time PCR: a new approach to the quantification of mitochondrial DNA damage and repair. (http://www.ncbi.nlm.nih.gov/pmc/articles/PMC1851651/) Retrieved 29 Nov 2011

141 Rein G, *The Body Quantum: Non-classical Behavior of Biological Systems,* "The Resonance in Residence Science Addendum," Ilonka Harezi, 2002.

142 Pert C, *Molecules of Emotion; The Science Behind Mind-Body Medicine,* (Touchstone, 1999), p. 23

143 Ibid., p.24

144 Pert C., *Your Body is Your Subconscious Mind, Study Guide,* (Sounds True, 2000), p. 7

145 Pert C, *Molecules of Emotion; The Science Behind Mind-Body Medicine,* (Touchstone, 1999), p. 186-187

146 Estés C P, *Women Who Run With Wolves; Myths and Stories of the Wild Woman Archetype,* (Ballantine Books, 1992), p. 336

147 Pert C, *Molecules of Emotion; The Science Behind Mind-Body Medicine,* (Touchstone, 1999), p. 143

148 Ibid., p.289

149 Ibid.

150 Hamer R G, *Summary of the New Medicine*, (Amici di Dirk, 2000)

151 Redpath W, *Trauma Energetics: a Study of Held-Energy Systems*, (Barberry Press, 1995)

152 Jal al-Dn Rm, *Maulana, The Glance: Rumi's Songs of Soul-Meeting*, Trans. Coleman Barks, Penguin Compass, 1999, p. 90

153 Pert C, *Molecules of Emotion; The Science Behind Mind-Body Medicine*, (Touchstone, 1999), p. 263

154 Light travels 19.557 times around the median circumference of Mercury per second.

155 Martineau J, *A Little Book of Coincidence*, (Walker & Company, 2002), p. 20

156 Martineau J, *A Little Book of Coincidence*, (Walker & Company, 2002), p. 41

157 Burnham S, *The Art of Intuition: Cultivating Your Inner Wisdom*, (Tarcher/Penguin, 2011), p. 149

158 Ibid.

159 c.1300, vtaues (pl., from popular O.Fr. form otaves), later reformed, from M.L. octava, from L. octava dies "eighth day," fem. of octavus "eighth," from octo. Originally "period of eight days after a festival," also "eighth day after a festival" (counting both days, thus if the festival was on a Sunday, the octaves would be the following Sunday). Verse sense of "stanza of eight lines" is from 1580s; musical sense of "note eight diatonic degrees above (or below) a given note" is first recorded 1650s, from L. octava (pars) "eighth part." (http://www.etymonline.com/index.php?term=octave) Online Etymology Dictionary. Retrieved Dec 6, 2011

160 Aubele T, Wenck S, Reynolds S, *Train Your Brain to Get Happy: The Simple Program That Primes Your Grey Cells for Joy, Optimism, and Serenity*, (Adams Media, 2011), p. 38

161 Ibid.

162 The actual quote is: ". . . what is man in the midst of nature? A nothing in comparison with the infinite, an all in comparison with nothingness: a mean between nothing and all.

References

Infinitely far from comprehending the extremes, the end of things and their principle are for him inevitably concealed in an impenetrable secret; equally incapable of seeing the nothingness whence he is derived, and the infinity in which he is swallowed up." The Thoughts, Letters and Opuscules of Blaise Pascal, O.W. Wright (trans.), (Hurd and Houghton, 1869), p. 160.

163 Fuller R B, *Synergetics: Explorations in the Geometry of Thinking*, (Macmillan Publishing Company, 1978), p. 116

164 At Jesus Christ's last supper, there were thirteen people around the table, counting Christ and the twelve apostles.

In Judaism, 13 signifies the age at which a boy matures and becomes a Bar Mitzvah.

In the Mayan Tzolk'in calendar, trecenas mark cycles of 13 day periods.

There are 13 cards in a suit.

The number of colonies that formed the United States.

165 Crossing the Event Horizon, www.theresonanceproject. org

166 Winfree A T, *When Time Breaks Down: The Three Dimensional Dynamics of Electrochemical Waves and Cardiac Arrhythmias*, (Princeton Press, 1986)

167 Ibid.

168 Pearce J C, *The Biology of Transcendence: A Blueprint of the Human Spirit*, (Park Street Press, 2004), p. 58

169 Goswami A, *How Quantum Activism Can Save Civilization*, (Hampton Roads Publishing Company, 2011), p. 53

170 *The Quantum Activist*, Film Documentary, 2009

171 Ibid.

172 Ibid.

173 Shabistari M, *Garden of Mystery (The Gulshan-i rāz of Mahmud Shabistari)*, Trans. Robert Abdul Hayy Darr, (Archetype, 2007), p. 66

174 Armour J, Ardell J. *Neurocardiology*. New York: Oxford University Press, 1994

Scalar Heart Connection™

175 McCraty R, *The Energetic Heart: Bioelectromagnetic Interactions Within and Between People*, (Institute of HeartMath, 2003), p. 3

176 An optimal level of heart-rate variability (HRV) is key to cardiovascular function, flexibility, and adaptability. Reduced HRV can be pathological. Heart-rhythm coherence refers to an orderly and harmonious organization of rhythms in information processing. See The Coherent Heart; Heart-Brain Interactions, Psychophysiological Coherence, and the Emergence of System-Wide Oder, by Rollin McCraty, Ph.D., Mike Atkinson, Dana Tomasino, and Raymond Trevor Bradley, Ph.D. (Institute of HeartMath, 2006).

177 Salovey P, Rothman A, Detweiler J, Steward W. Emotional states and physical health. *Am Psychol* 2000; 55; 110-121

178 Goswami A, *How Quantum Activism Can Save Civilization*, (Hampton Roads Publishing Company, 2011), p. 82

179 Ibid., p. 80

180 Jung C G, Synchronicity: An Acausal Connecting Principle, from Vol. 8. of the Collected Works of C. G. Jung, (Princeton University Press, 2010), par. 865, p. 36

181 Jung C G, forward to *The I-Ching* Trans. Wilhelm R, Bollingen Series XIX (Princeton University Press, 1997), p. xxv

182 Jung C G, *Synchronicity: An Acausal Connecting Principle*, from Vol. 8. of the Collected Works of C. G. Jung, (Princeton University Press, 2010), p. 40

183 Laurence Hecht, *Advances in Developing the Moon Nuclear Model*, 21st Century, Fall 2000

184 Xavier Borg, The Particle – The wrong turn that led physics to a dead end, Blaze Labs Research, (http://blazelabs.com/f-p-develop.asp). Retrieved 09 Nov 2011

185 Maria Göeppert-Mayer, The Shell Model, Nobel Lecture, December 12, 1963

186 Marie-Louise von Franz, *Number and Time*, (Northwestern University Press, 1998), p. 47

187 Xavier Borg, The Particle – The wrong turn that led phys-

References

ics to a dead end, Blaze Labs Research, (http://blazelabs.
com/f-p-magic.asp). Retrieved 09 Nov 2011
188 Ibid.15

Resources

Basic for Every Heart Workshop

Your heart will always tell you what you need to know. You only need to know how to ask and how to listen.

Join us for a day of fun experiencing conversations with your own heart. Hear what your heart has to say about what prevents you from experiencing joy and inner connection and harmony.

Scalar Heart Connection™ is a simple and easy technique designed to quickly bring unconscious negative beliefs to conscious awareness so we can release them and remove them one by one from the translucent walls of the royal chamber of our heart.

This workshop will teach you how to identify what is preventing you from experiencing what you want and deserve. Most importantly, it will teach you how to entrain the resonance of your desires into patterns that attract what is life enhancing. You will learn how to use this process on yourself and how you can apply it with your loved ones.

Learn and experience Scalar Heart Connection™, a method to help bring human beings into greater harmony within themselves and with the planet as a whole. This is the beginning of a new chapter in the evolution of what it means to be human in your life and in the life of others.

To register or for more information:

www.ScalarHeartConnection.com

Resources

"I was particularly impressed by the explanation of the Scalar Heart Connection™ and the invitation to move the energy potential into action through our intention. I found this workshop to be informative and inspirational and I experienced it as supportive of life on all levels."
~ Jennifer J.

"This was a fascinating study of how universal archetypes and numbers can combine with intuition and sound vibration. I've always wondered how all of these elements come together. I loved the workshop. It was food for mind and soul and was emotionally satisfying. It gave me major insight into an emotional block."
~ Amber D.

"This is an amazing way of getting to the true me. It was hard for me to share in front of the group, but I am glad I did. This workshop helped me a lot."
~ Laura W.

"Wow, I had a real revelation connecting my birth to my issue."
~ Janice S.

"I do similar work to help folks identify negative core beliefs and then re-decide. It appears that this work can accomplish the same thing in a much simpler and faster way. I am truly optimistic!"
~ Tracy S.

"Amazing, interesting, NEW way of looking at things. I learned a lot and enjoyed it immensely."
~ Susan L.

Scalar Heart Connection™

"Stephen's presentation takes deeply profound material and presents it in a clean, calm, and simple way. This is the mark of mastery. His calm, peaceful presence and the presence of his beautiful family was deeply nourishing."
~ Debra B.

Also available:
* CD – Scalar Heart Connection™ Meditation
* CD – Quantum Healing Codes™

www.ScalarHeartConnection.com